STANDA

'It is a myth that childhood is always happy for there is much to frighten, frustrate and humiliate the growing young person.'

Although stress is now regarded as a major health problem and many books on stress control have been written for adults, there is no comparable book on ways of introducing children to methods of relaxation at home and at school.

This unique book shows how parents, teachers and social workers can help children to discover methods of coping with stress. The skill of relaxation applied to everyday living situations will not only help them during the stresses of childhood but will become a skill of value for the rest of life, a real aid towards mental and physical health.

All the techniques are illustrated by 100 informative and enchanting photographs of children enjoying learning to relax at home and in school.

Jane Madders is a qualified teacher of physical education and is a chartered physiotherapist. She was also head of department for health education and school counselling at the city of Birmingham teacher training college. She has taught in child guidance clinics dealing with nervous and over-active children and has held classes for migraine sufferers. She has taught relaxation to students and staff at Birmingham University.

Jane Madders is the author of many books including *Stress and Relaxation* which has been translated into many languages. She has also appeared both on radio and television.

RELAX AND BE HAPPY

Jane Madders

UNWIN PAPERBACKS

London   Boston   Sydney

First published by Unwin Paperbacks 1987

UNWIN PAPERBACKS
A Division of Unwin Hyman Ltd
40 Museum Street, London WC1A 1LU, UK

Unwin Paperbacks
A Division of Unwin Hyman Ltd
Park Lane, Hemel Hempstead, Herts HP2 4TE, UK

Allen & Unwin Australia Pty Ltd
8 Napier Street, North Sydney, NSW 2060, Australia

Unwin Paperbacks with the Port Nicholson Press, PO Box 11-838 Wellington, New Zealand

© Jane Madders 1987

British Library Cataloguing in Publication Data

Madders, Jane
    Relax and be happy.
1. Stress in children
I. Title
155.4   BF723.S75
ISBN 0–04–649043–4

Designed by Behram Kapadia

Set in 11 on 13 point Garamond by Nene Phototypesetters Ltd, Northampton and printed in Great Britain

Contents

Preface *page* 7

1 The cycle of stress and distress   10

2 Recognising signs of stress   23

3 Self-help relaxation   26

4 The role of parents and teachers   30

5 Techniques of relaxation   38
    Early school years   43
    Middle years of childhood   73
    Teenagers and students   89

6 Suggested study routines for students   108

7 Calming massage   115

Appendices
    1 Suggestions for music for dance   135
    2 Some other methods   137
    3 Further reading   139
    4 Useful addresses   143

Acknowledgements

My thanks go to all the children who so enthusiastically acted as models for the photographs and to the teachers who tried out the techniques in their schools. Ron Swift, assisted by his daughter Caroline, took the delightful photographs and made the sessions enjoyable for us all. I am grateful to Amber Lloyd, the Hon. Secretary of Relaxation for Living, for persuading me to make a cassette on relaxation for children: this and requests from adults attending relaxation classes led me to write this book.

I had much help and support from Dr Janek Wankowski, educational guidance counsellor at Birmingham University. Others who gave me assistance include inspectors of physical education in London and Birmingham, Lynn Howell and Liz Perkins of the Birmingham Health Education Department, the tutors of the Health Education Council's LOOK AFTER YOURSELF courses, staff at the Centre for Child Study and the Physical Education Department at Birmingham University, John Handley who shared his research on children's posture and good body use, Pat Van Zyl, and many parents belonging to the National Childbirth Trust. Martin Dunitz gave permission for the Stop Emergency technique from *Stress and Relaxation* to be included.

I owe much of the section on children's needs and when to seek help to the late Dr Kellmer Pringle, who lectured to my students and later became the director of the National Children's Bureau.

My thanks also go to Emma and Tom, our grandchildren, who keep my feet firmly on the ground, but allow me to share their exciting world of adventure and new ideas.

Preface

Children who are coping well are usually happy, and the overall pattern of childhood is one of joy, fun, curiosity and zest for living. But all children have to contend with stress: whether they are tough or timid, aggressive or withdrawn, intelligent or dull they, like adults, have to meet stress head on every day. Because they are immature, have only a limited experience, are passing through periods of rapid change and are much at the mercy of grown-ups, they are particularly vulnerable. If you doubt whether children can suffer from the effects of stress, you must have forgotten your own childhood. We all bear scars from our earlier fears, humiliations and frustrations, and some of these will have lasting effects on personality and behaviour.

The aim of this book is to help parents and teachers introduce to children and young adults some techniques of relaxation which will help them manage reasonable stress and tension, and enable them to take some responsibility for their own feelings. It can encourage a positive attitude to mental and physical health and will become a skill of value throughout life. Children who are seriously disturbed, though, will require expert help with behaviour, cognitive or other therapy, and this book is not concerned with these therapeutic measures but with preventive ones. However, even unhappy and distressed children will benefit from learning how to relax as part of their therapy.

Adults attending relaxation classes often remark how much they wish they had learnt these calming methods in childhood. Although anyone at any age can learn to relax, it is very difficult for adults to change attitudes and alter long-held habits of over-reacting, over-arousal, and prolonged muscle tension. It is in childhood that ways of relaxing can most easily be learnt.

During the past two decades there has been an alarming increase in the use of mood changing drugs: tranquillisers, sedatives and anti-depressants, not only by adults but sometimes prescribed for children. There is growing concern about the ill-effects of their long-term use and this has led many adults to seek a self-help method to help them cope with stress and tension without using drugs. There are a number of well proven self-help methods, some centuries old, others just emerging, and some incorporating modern technology. All these systems involve muscle relaxation, either directly or indirectly, and there is now plenty of evidence to show that this simple technique – learnt as a physical skill and then applied to daily living situations – can be remarkably effective on its own. It involves no drugs, is wholly under the control of the individual and, like most physical skills, it is best learnt in childhood.

I was fortunate when I was a student at a physical education college because we were taught relaxation as an integral part of the course, and every gymnastics and dance lesson ended with a short spell of general relaxation. Later, during my physiotherapy training, every student was tested to show that she could relax muscles at will. This was because massage was at that time an important part of therapy, and for it to be effective both the patient and therapist must be able to relax. Although we lacked the advantages of modern electrical apparatus, we did learn to develop sensitivity in our hands and discover how effective massage can be in reducing anxiety and tension.

Since qualifying as a teacher and physiotherapist I have taught relaxation as part of physical education to children of all ages, to disturbed children in child guidance clinics, to mothers in ante- and post-natal classes, and more recently to staff and students at the university and teacher training college where I was lecturer in Health Education and Child Development. I also held relaxation classes at the Birmingham Migraine clinic. All these experiences helped me to adapt my methods and I learnt a lot from them all.

It may seem surprising that a book on relaxation pays so much attention to exercise and activity. These are important because they have a profound influence on children's feelings of well-being and confidence. When I worked in the child guidance clinics I discovered how closely self-esteem in children is related to physical prowess. Many of these children were timid, anxious, some afraid of school and some were stammerers. Many, especially the boys, were less competent at physical skills than their peers and were rejected by them. They were often prey to the school bullies and some were exhausted by their fears and tension, were frequently ill and school work was suffering. We found that by giving them opportunities to acquire physical skills like climbing, kicking a ball accurately, 'being brave' in dramatic situations, and then to learn some emergency relaxation techniques which they could use in a crisis, most of them gradually gained in self-esteem and learnt to manage their feelings. It was heart-warming to see them growing in confidence and often the teachers and parents noticed this change and were aware of the greater respect of the other children. Sometimes this success flowed over to their school work and teachers reported an improvement.

Other groups of children were over-active, presenting formidable problems for parents and teachers (and sometimes for me). Some were slightly brain-damaged, some may have been affected by dietary factors, but most of them were frustrated active children, denied opportunities to let off steam in an acceptable manner with vigorous physical activity. They were often alarmed by their own explosive behaviour and scared by their lack of control over their feelings. These children responded well to directed strenuous activity, and this was always followed by spells of relaxation and tension control and some quieting mental imagery. A number of them came to enjoy feelings of self-induced quiet and calm and their movements became more controlled. As a result of these experiences I include in this book some vigorous fun activities as a prelude to relaxation for young children.

My work with migraine sufferers included an investigation into the effects of relaxation on patients whose high levels of arousal were considered to be the main factor in precipitating their attacks. The results were encouraging.

They taught me that relaxation on its own is not sufficient. In addition to daily practice, it must become part of everyday living: recognising unnecessary muscle tension, becoming aware of the kind of situations that produced their stress reaction and learning to substitute a relaxation response instead. So in this book I have indicated some situations where relaxation can be useful in everyday situations.

In the classes for mothers with young children, an exercise session was followed by relaxation and ended with discussions on various aspects of family life. It soon became evident that many of their problems and anxieties arose from their lack of knowledge of what are the normal stages of development of children. Parents often expect standards of behaviour which are inappropriate for the age and maturity of the child – I know, I did this myself – so I have given a profile of a child of each age group in the section on techniques of relaxation. (However there are always individual differences in children, so don't worry if yours doesn't fit; there is no such thing as a 'typical' child.)

Working with students made me more aware of the escalating pressures of present-day academic demands and the social problems of living away from home and the support of a good school. Birmingham was the first university to undertake systematic research into students' learning difficulties. A report was published, *Students: why some fail* written by Dr J. Wankowski, the educational guidance counsellor. He has helped many students to understand the emotional undercurrents of learning and to acquire more effective methods of study. I have included some of his suggestions for study as well as some relaxation techniques for students.

I have enjoyed writing this book. It sums up many happy memories of working with children and adults. It recalls much of the warmth, the fun, and the sharing of successes we enjoyed together. There were some children I could not help, and they taught me my limitations.

Upon a special birthday of mine, my little granddaughter brought me a charming posy of flowers. She explained that although she hadn't grown them all by herself, she had chosen and picked them, and that the ribbon they were tied up with was her own. There have been many wise teachers over the centuries whose ideas have influenced my teaching. I too have chosen some, rejected or adapted others. But it is my own ribbon of experience that binds them together in this book.

1
The cycle of stress and distress

What is stress?

The word 'stress' is often used loosely and inappropriately, and because its meaning is so imprecise and vague the medical profession is reluctant to use it. Doctors talk instead about 'levels of arousal' and this is quite useful because 'to arouse' means to stir up, to become active, and this is just what the body does when it goes into action to deal with problems. Others talk of 'effort', and this is useful too because it indicates the striving that is necessary for efficiency and achievement.

However, I shall continue to use the word stress because it makes sense to most people, and I will try to describe just what I mean by it.

'Stress' is a term which was originally used in physics and engineering where it means the physical pressure exerted upon or between parts of a body. When deformation occurs as a result it is called strain. This partly describes what happens to human beings when they experience undue stress and strain at work or at home.

Hans Selye, the widely acclaimed authority on the physiology of stress, describes it as: 'the response of the body to any demand made upon it', and 'the rate of wear and tear on the body'. Life is a process of adaptation to the internal and external changes we encounter every day, and stress is the bodily reaction that enables us to adapt and survive. So the definition I shall use for the basis of this book is this.

> Stress is the effort used to stir up the body to adapt to change. It is a reaction that prepares the body for vigorous action when danger threatens, whether the cause is real or imaginary.

This indicates that it is a healthy and valuable response necessary for survival, but that the reaction can be produced for something that is not an actual danger to life but may be imaginary: being fearful about a forthcoming event, recalling an alarming experience, or just a threat to our self-esteem. It is not the situation itself that causes the ill-effects of stress, but the way we react to it. By understanding something about the nature of stress and becoming tuned in to our bodily responses to it, we can discover how much we can cope with and find ways of exerting some control over our stress reactions. We don't have to be the helpless victims of our emotional and physical reactions and the illnesses that stress can generate, and we can help our children to develop an understanding of ways in which they can use stress to their advantage. By taking some responsibility for their own well-being they can learn to enjoy the zest of life and experience positive stress without distress.

The positive aspects of stress

Stress can be fun, an exciting challenge that gives us the necessary kick to get us going. When it is well-managed it becomes the spur to action and is essential for success at work and in sport.

We know that a measure of anxiety improves learning, and acceptable pressures can be creative, leading to excellent and original work. This kind of stress becomes the nudge that pushes us on to achieve more. It is the same with sport; athletes and players of competitive games are increasingly aware of the value of generating a suitable amount of arousal in order to reach peak performance. Many coaches are now introducing methods of 'psyching up' or 'tensing up' into their training programmes and combining these with relaxation and visualisation techniques.

Hans Selye uses the word 'Eustress' to describe positive and pleasant stress – this derives from the Greek 'eu' meaning good and pleasant. The bodily reactions for positive stress are the same as those for unpleasant negative stress, but provided they are kept within bounds they appear to be less harmful.

Tension in itself is not undesirable and can be useful and enjoyable. An early morning dip in the sea or lake causes strong tension but can be an invigorating experience for the healthy person. From the first toe testing to the breathtaking plunge into cold water the stress factors of the body are at work. But soon there is the whole body-mind exhilaration and subsequent feelings of well-being and relaxation – at least for some people. For those terrified of the water, it would be sheer horrifying distress.

However, overcoming this and other fears can create positive and useful stress too. I know many children who were very scared of the water but managed to learn to swim. Their overwhelming joy and pride when they swam the first few strokes was evident. Success breeds success and the feelings of achievement and self-respect spread over to work at school.

Many educationalists recognise the benefits of adventure courses for young people where, under careful guidance, they develop self-reliance and discover inner resources. They learn to cope positively with stress and gain self-respect.

I can understand that some forms of stress release hormones which have exhilarating effects, and that some people can even become addicted to these hormone reactions. When I was a student I took part in mountain climbing. On one occasion the climb was difficult and frightening; half way up I became frozen with fear, trembling, tearful and too terrified to go on. I was skilfully coaxed on and up, and when I reached the top, the relief of tension and the breathtaking view over the mountains resulted in unparalleled feelings of exhilaration. Moreover it gave me more confidence in my ability to cope with fear in more ordinary situations and remains a treasured memory. This was sufficient for me, but recent studies have shown that some people get hooked on the exhilarating sensations they get when stress hormones are released when activities are very strenuous or alarming.

Most normal children enjoy being a little frightened especially when they feel generally secure. We may be alarmed at their avid enjoyment of grisly tales, their games of dares, telling ghost stories in all their gory details, their enjoyment of scary films but if we are truthful we can remember doing this ourselves. It is part of growing up and becomes a practice of coping with fear while they are in a secure environment.

Too little stress is harmful

Children need a reasonable amount of stress to function properly. It should never be more than they can manage in the light of their age, experience and personality, but sameness and too little change can be harmful. All children have a natural curiosity and eagerly seek new experiences. If they are denied sufficient mental and physical stimulation with the resultant feelings of self-esteem and self-confidence they may either become listless, apathetic and bored, or else they may seek over-stimulation in socially unacceptable ways: very loud music, vandalism, violence, cruelty. There are of course other reasons for these disturbances, but lack of suitable rewarding stimulation and the resulting boredom and frustration is a major cause. Children need a reasonable amount of stress to function properly, but not more than they can manage.

Too little stress or too much stress will lead to distress.

Children and stress

No one, from birth to old age, can escape from the effects of stress. It is part of living and, like grown-ups, children have their own way of interpreting what is alarming to them and their own way of reacting to it.

Every child is unique, unprecedented and unrepeatable, the result of an intricate interplay between inherited characteristics and all the physical and emotional experiences that have happened from conception onwards. Because of this, each child will respond differently to stress. Some react more sensitively to everything: to them the world is a noisier, smellier, brighter, more alarming and stimulating place than it is to others. They are bombarded with sensations and are alert and on guard all the time. Others seem to take life more stolidly, rarely get excited, take disapproval in their stride and often need a good push to get them going at anything demanding. These are not better or worse children, and it is no use parents wasting energy feeling guilty about this. They just are different, and some are more vulnerable than others, though all of them have a breaking point. We cannot expect each child to tolerate the same amount of stress as others, and a situation which may be frightening to one may be sheer fun to another.

Children cannot be treated all in the same way and we have to respect their uniqueness. This presents great problems to teachers, especially when they have to deal with large numbers of children. In one of my classes I could be angry with one tough disruptive boy knowing well that he would respond with good-humoured tolerance, accept my anger as one of my foibles and get on with his work untroubled. But it was the little quiet boy in the corner I had to watch at the same time. Whenever anyone displayed anger, even when it was nothing to do with him, he would go so pale with fright that his ears became almost transparent. I could not treat him in the same way: for him a slight gesture was enough.

But although we have to try to treat children differently, they long to be the same as others: they do not wish to be different. It is a source of stress to them to be noticeably unlike their peers, to have different clothes, hairstyles, possessions, to have a 'funny accent', be a different colour, have an obvious blemish, and even having unusual parents can be shameful. This longing to be the same can sometimes lead to behaviour which may be uncharacteristic of the child's usual behaviour. In my group of stammerers at the child guidance clinic, I had a timid, gentle, anxious boy who gradually became more confident in the lively activity sessions. One day his mother reported to me that he had been punished in school because he had cheeked the teacher. She was upset by this, but my reaction was of delight: here was the first sign that he was getting better. He had been brave enough to be slightly impertinent, he had managed to find the words to say, and even more important to him perhaps, he had, like other boys, received punishment for his minor misconduct. He was no longer different.

Not only do children react in their own special way to situations, but their bodies respond differently too. Stress can spark off many disorders especially if there is already an inherited proneness to a particular illness and this will differ from child to child. Behaviour reactions may be different also: one may become tense and withdrawn with anxiety while another may have bursts of aggression.

We are beginning to know much more about the factors which influence the growth and development of children. A long-term research study of thousands of children from birth to adulthood by the National Children's Bureau indicates that there is now plenty of evidence to show that a significant proportion of children suffer from behavioural and emotional problems in their school years, and that many children suffer from stress disorders of sufficient severity to handicap them in their everyday life.

Boys in general were found to react differently to stress from girls.

They more often responded with aggression and disobedience, became more restless and found it difficult to settle to anything for more than a few moments. They were more readily picked out as being disruptive and troubled than girls who more often reacted by being miserable, tearful, biting their nails and becoming faddy about food, and their signals of distress were less easily noticed.

Some children suffer intensely. It is a myth that childhood is altogether a happy phase of life, for there is much to frustrate, frighten and humiliate the growing child. Some anxieties are common to all children, from the young child's fears of being abandoned or rejected by parents, to starting school, being ridiculed by adults or other children, not being accepted by their peers, to the escalating pressures of examinations, competitions, finding a job and coping with sex. In addition, many young people nowadays are over stimulated with scaring videos, very loud music, discos with flashing lights, and magazines of violence and sadism.

Research has shown that children living in large cities have a higher incidence of stress disorders than children in rural areas and there is no doubt that many youngsters maintain a high level of arousal much more often and for much longer than they should.

Ratings of stressful events by a group of junior-age children

A group of junior-age children and parents rated a number of stressful events in order of severity. Although there was a slight variation between boys' and girls' assessments, in general they were in agreement. You may find that you and your children rate these differently or would add other items.

The list is in order of severity, the most stressful first.

Loss of a parent (death or divorce)
Wetting in class
Getting lost; being left alone in the house
Bullied by older children
Picked last for the team
Ridiculed in class
Parental rows
Moving to a new class or school
Going to the dentist; going to hospital
Tests and exams
Taking a bad report home
Breaking or losing things
Being different (accent, clothes, parents, size)
New baby in the family
Performing in public (music, plays, sport)
Being late for school
Anticipating exciting events (Christmas, parties, holidays, treats)

A lifestyle index for older children and students

Most of our really stressful experiences come from a change in lifestyle. Two doctors at the University of Washington, Thomas Holmes and Richard Rahe, developed a Life Change Index, tested it with a large number of adults and found that those who scored highly stood a good chance of having a major illness within a year. A Canadian fitness group 'Action BC' drew up an index for older children and the following is a list slightly amended for British older children. A score of fifty in a six-month period is considered to be stressful enough to cause illness.

The list begins with the most stressful.

	SCORE
Death of a parent	50
Death of a close relative	40
Loss of a parent through divorce	35
Death of a close friend	30
Parents having rows or in financial trouble	28
Serious health problems, surgery, pregnancy	25
Engagement or marriage	25
Conflict with parents	23
In trouble with the law	22
Unemployed, financial trouble	19
Break up with boy or girl friend	19
Interviews or starting a new job	18
Insecurity about future	18
Sexual difficulties	18
Not part of the crowd	16
Lack of privacy	15
Driving test	15
School pressures, exams, deadlines	15
Difficulty in making decisions	14
Concern about appearance, weight, identity	13
Recent move, home, school, college	11
Lack of recognition	9
General feelings of frustration	6

Although life change is not something to avoid, too much change in a short time increases the risk of health problems. So try to spread out the changes wherever possible, and use relaxation techniques to minimise the effects.

The cycle of stress and distress

Distress occurs when high levels of arousal caused by anxiety, excitement or apprehension are maintained for too long and become more than the child can manage. This can lead to distress with ill-health and behavioural problems.

Bodily changes as a result of stress

In order to understand how prolonged distress can lead to illness, and why relaxation techniques can be effective, it is a help to know a little about the bodily changes in stress and what happens when these are prolonged. Older children will find this interesting because it is a fascinating aspect of the wonderful way the body works to maintain its balance while it adapts to changing situations, and it also explains how we can hinder its smooth working.

Like all animals, human beings have an in-built survival mechanism which enables them to act swiftly and vigorously in an emergency when life is threatened. Immediately the danger is recognised the body prepares for physical exertion to get ready for the three 'F's: Fight, Flight, or if neither is possible, to Freeze.

The part of the brain which sets everything in motion is the hypothalamus (if you were to stick your fingers in your ears, where they would meet in the middle is about where it is situated). This is the centre for the emotions, and is concerned with the harmonious integration of all the systems of the body involved in maintaining the internal balance necessary for survival. It acts as a giant switchboard, receiving and sending messages to all the organs in the body.

When we are alarmed one of the first things to happen is the involuntary tightening of muscles. They go tense ready for action (and children especially may start to tremble, particularly the muscles round the mouth). At the same time there is a sharp intake of breath, a gasp, then the breath may be held for a while. Remember this first reaction of muscle tension and irregular breathing when we come to consider the role of relaxation and calm breathing in coping with stress.

The message of danger is received and immediately an astonishing series of reactions takes place, most of them in a split second. Hormones, the chemical messengers of the body, are poured into the bloodstream and they and nervous messages are sent to all systems of the body to prepare them for vigorous activity, to get ready for conflict. Priority needs are for muscles, heart and brain, so blood is diverted to them from other parts of the body which can go without for the emergency. So the skin goes pale as blood vessels constrict (this may also have a useful purpose in limiting bleeding from superficial wounds in fighting). In anger, the skin may flush with rage. Digestion is not important for the emergency period so the blood supply to the stomach and intestines is temporarily shut down. Even the capillaries in the kidneys constrict.

The increased blood and oxygen supply to the muscles is necessary because muscle energy depends on fuel in the form of blood sugar, and it requires oxygen to transform the sugar into energy and these are transported in the bloodstream to the muscles. Later, fats are released into the bloodstream from stores in many parts of the body and oxygen is again required for the chemical reaction which transforms the fats to produce energy. In order to get the blood to the muscles the heart has to beat faster and more strongly, blood pressure rises and we may be aware of the fast thumping heart beat. In order to provide the necessary extra oxygen, the lungs work harder and breathing is faster and gasping.

The adrenal glands stimulate the body to its maximum efficiency to meet the potential danger and release the stress hormones adrenaline and noradrenaline; these produce different reactions though they both prepare the body for action. Adrenaline is more likely to be associated with anxiety, and noradrenaline with anger, frustration and excitement and is said to be responsible for the feelings of euphoria associated with distance jogging, and strenuous frightening activities like mountaineering or rough sailing.

Other changes occur almost simultaneously: the mouth goes dry as the salivary glands shut down, the pupils of the eyes dilate so that vision is better in the dark or half light, the liver releases its store of sugar into the bloodstream, the spleen discharges its concentration of blood corpuscles, breathing becomes faster and deeper, sweating occurs to enable the body to cool down during vigorous activity. The blood is enabled to clot more easily to prevent serious blood loss and promote healing. The immune system, a most remarkable defensive mechanism of the body which is normally concerned with resisting and overcoming disease, is damped down for the emergency situation: it has no useful purpose during the short-lived vigorous preparation for conflict.

All these and many other changes are part of the remarkable ability of the body to adapt for survival. Then when vigorous activity (like winning the fight or escaping) has used up the biochemicals of stress and the physical changes are no longer necessary, the body returns quickly to normal and no harm is done. Feelings of relaxation, and sometimes of exhilaration, are part of the reward.

What happens when the child's stress reactions are prolonged

There are not many occasions in civilised and urban life when vigorous physical action is the answer to a stressful situation. Your child can produce these reactions for something that is not a danger to life but to his self-respect, or for intense excitement over a long period, anxiety about a forthcoming event, for noises in the dark. When these are short-lived, no harm is done and the body quickly returns to normal. But when the reactions are prolonged, or very intense and inappropriate, the child's whole body can be upset.

Disorders associated with stress

Illness, with corresponding physical and mental changes, may occur if the cycle of stress moves on to distress. It is important though to note that stress is not the only cause. It is the combination of a predisposition to the disorder together with stress that triggers off the illness. There is often a family pattern of proneness to a particular disorder.

BREATHING   Hyperventilation – if breathing remains rapid and in excess of the body's needs there may be fainting, giddiness, feelings of panic and in vulnerable children it may spark off attacks of asthma and other respiratory disorders.

DIGESTION   If the digestive system remains without its proper blood supply there may be tummy upsets, vomiting, colitis.

ELIMINATION   The bladder and bowel muscles may loosen so that the child may have fequent urination ('wetting pants with fright'), diarrhoea or sometimes constipation.

SKIN   If skin changes persist the child may sweat profusely, especially in adolescence. In vulnerable children there may be skin allergies, eczema, rashes.

Figure 1   Common disorders associated with stress

PREDISPOSITION   STRESS

SICK HEADACHES, MIGRAINE
BREATHING DIFFICULTIES, ASTHMA
GASTRIC UPSETS, DIARRHOEA
DIABETES
SKIN RASHES, ECZEMA
LESSENED IMMUNITY

IMPORTANT NOTE

It is not stress alone that causes the attacks. The gun is loaded when the child is born with a proneness to the particular disorder. Stress is the trigger that sets it off.

IMMUNE SYSTEM   If the immune system remains damped down the child will not be able to withstand infections and may have frequent minor illnesses.

BLOOD VESSEL CHANGES   The change in blood vessels may cause headaches.

MOUTH   If the mouth remains dry the child will find little interest in eating and may have difficulty in swallowing. Some children develop mouth ulcers when they have been troubled for some time.

VISION   If the pupils remain dilated, vision may become blurred.

SLEEP DISTURBANCE   The high level of arousal may interfere with sleep. The child may be too excited or anxious to go to sleep, but when he or she does there may be scary nightmares. (Most children will have these sometimes but stress makes it worse.)

REPRODUCTIVE SYSTEM   The menstrual cycle may be delayed. Dysmenorrhoea (painful periods) or pre-menstrual tension may be made worse by stress.

MUSCLE TENSION   Long-held muscle tension may produce vague aches and pains in muscles and tension will interfere with fine muscle movements, such as writing when the pen is held too tightly. Excessive muscle tension hinders good musical performance and athletic skills. The child can become fatigued and thin as a result of unnecessary and excessive effort.

LEARNING   Children under stress often show difficulties of concentration and comprehension.

BEHAVIOUR   Irritability and problem behaviour may occur.

SENSITISATION TO STRESS   If these stress changes persist for a long time, some children become so sensitised that everything appears alarming, the slightest noise makes them jump and they become worried about everything. Some even become deeply depressed. In this way the cycle from healthy stress to distress is complete.

NOTE It is worth repeating that stress is not the only cause of these disorders and medical advice should be sought if the symptoms appear to be serious.

Stress can affect learning

Although an increase in effort improves performance, if it is increased beyond a certain limit, efficiency drops. Over-anxiety acts as a block to understanding, disrupts efficient learning, and the resultant failure may cause the child or student to lose all interest in academic work.

Most adults can recall the long-term effects of humiliation by a disliked or feared teacher and how this inhibited interest in the subject. On the other hand we may joyfully remember how we were influenced by someone who fanned a weak flame of interest into an abiding fire of enthusiasm.

Breaking the cycle

The cycle can be broken at several points. Some will require intervention and support by adults, but some (C and D below) can be under the child's own control. The chapters on techniques give ideas on how this may be achieved.

Help from adults

A Change the situation; give the child a breathing space – a holiday, perhaps a break from home, sometimes works wonders; it gives the child and parent some respite, and during the usual school vacation the child has time to grow up a little and become more able to cope. More drastic measures are sometimes necessary: changing school, avoiding the stressful situations like social occasions, examinations, competitions, rather than face them. (Sometimes this may be the only answer if things have got very bad, but is only a last resort. It is worth considering but get expert advice about this.)

B Change the mental attitude towards the situation – is it really alarming?

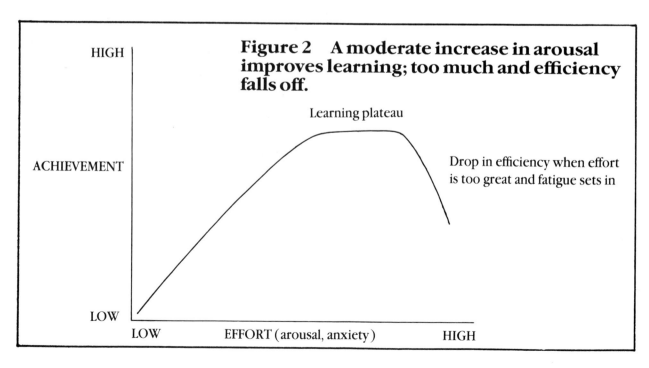

Figure 2   A moderate increase in arousal improves learning; too much and efficiency falls off.

Learning plateau

Drop in efficiency when effort is too great and fatigue sets in

HIGH

ACHIEVEMENT

LOW

LOW   EFFORT (arousal, anxiety)   HIGH

Parents and teachers can help by giving the child confidence, by boosting up self-esteem, talking over problems and giving support throughout the stressful experience. The 'mental shrug' is a recognition that the situation does not warrant a stress reaction, so it is shrugged off. Habituation means that by getting used to the situation the stress diminishes.

Self-help methods

C   Change the bodily reactions; substitute a relaxation response for the tension.

D   Take exercise; use up the bodily stress reactions by vigorous activity.

Parents and teachers can teach these self-help methods to children and encourage their use in coping with stress.

Figure 3 The cycle of stress and distress

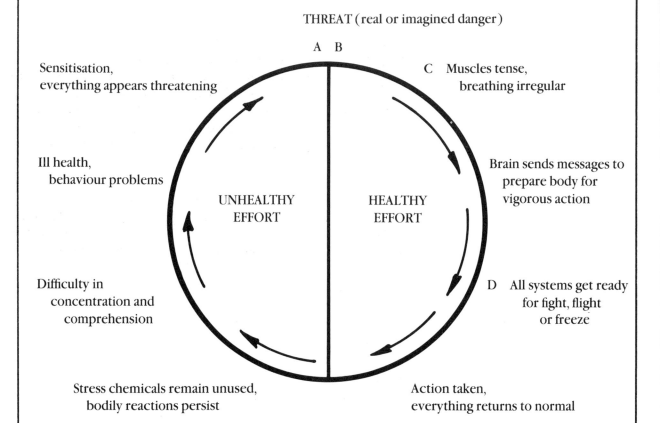

THREAT (real or imagined danger)

A B

Sensitisation,
everything appears threatening

C Muscles tense,
breathing irregular

Ill health,
behaviour problems

Brain sends messages to
prepare body for
vigorous action

UNHEALTHY
EFFORT

HEALTHY
EFFORT

Difficulty in
concentration and
comprehension

D All systems get ready
for fight, flight
or freeze

Stress chemicals remain unused,
bodily reactions persist

Action taken,
everything returns to normal

THE CYCLE CAN BE BROKEN AT SEVERAL POINTS

A Change or avoid the situation.
B Change mental attitude: Is it really alarming? The 'mental shrug'.
   Get used to it (habituation).
C Change bodily reaction: substitute a relaxation response.
D Use up stress chemicals: take exercise.

2

Recognising signs of stress

Children who are happy are usually coping well; they display an obvious sense of joy, fun, and zest for living. All children have times when they are unhappy and have difficulty in coping with problems, but most sort them out for themselves, especially if they are not badgered. However, if the child is continually unhappy, insecure, and failing in personal relationships it indicates that there may be more stress than the child can manage alone. It should not be difficult to spot this failing to cope when children are young: their feelings and emotions are near the surface. When young children are happy they jump for joy, their facial expression and posture show exactly how they feel. When they are sad, their faces and gestures tell the world. It is this whole person response that matters most, although there are some individual signs that may give clues.

Physical signs

Note that these may not always be warnings of stress, but can all become bad habits, so keep an eye on them.

Muscle tension
Hunched shoulders
Gripped hands, tapping fingers
Tense anxious forehead
Hair pulling
Thumb sucking
Nail biting, finger biting
Pen held tightly
Trembling, lip biting or sucking

Posture
Drooping posture of sadness
Tense uptight posture of apprehension
Hollow back of over-alertness

Breathing
Breathing faster than normal, high up in the chest
Sighing or gasping

Emotional signs and when to seek help

These criteria may help you to judge whether the child has more stress than can be managed without some help.

Consider the behaviour in the light of these observations:

Is this something that is normal for this stage of development? e.g. thumb sucking is common in 3-year-olds but not in 8-year-olds.

How intense is it? e.g. 90% of children bite their nails at some time, but if nails are bitten so much that injury occurs there may be trouble.

Does it occur frequently? e.g. occasional bedwetting is common but if this occurs every night after the age of six some help may be required.

Does it prevent the child doing the things he wants to? e.g. Is stammering or severe shyness preventing him from making friends?

Is the behaviour disrupting your life and that of others?

Is the behaviour bizarre, strange and unchildlike?

Some tell-tale signs

You will be unusually lucky if your child does not show one or two of these signs at some time or other, so don't worry, but if there are many disturbing pointers look at them in the light of the criteria above and the overall pattern of the child's behaviour. Then take action if necessary.

There are some emotional pointers. The parent or teacher may notice that the child is fearful of almost everything, is excessively withdrawn, unresponsive, with no interests, or may be sad and depressed. (Yes, children really can suffer from depression and may have long periods of melancholy.)

Unmanageable stress may show up in educational difficulties when the child falls well below his potential ability and there is a marked change in academic performance (and of course any child who is failing at school is bound to be disturbed when self-esteem is further damaged this way). Unhappy children find it hard to concentrate, and comprehension is impaired. They find it hard to listen and understand if they are preoccupied with their problems.

More easily noticed are the behavioural disorders like frequent rages and unmanageableness because they disturb the home and disrupt school. Some children may have sudden explosive and alarming bursts of hyperactivity and this may be related to frustration and stress. But sometimes it may be a bodily reaction to certain factors in diet. If you suspect this to be the case, try to get advice or gradually eliminate suspect foods especially those containing additives like tartrazine, the orange colouring. Notice any other foods that seem to spark off an attack, even sugar may be a culprit. But it's only a minority of children who suffer this way and it would be worth while getting in touch with a society concerned with hyperactive children to get more information and support. Persistent truancy and wandering away from home are signs that the child needs help. Drug taking and glue sniffing present a growing problem for parents and teachers and at first the signs are difficult to detect. Look out for stains around the mouth and on the clothes and there may be unusual smells. Or scorched tinfoil and odd capsules may be left around. There is usually a marked deterioration in work, health and general behaviour. These drug abusers are often furtive and evasive, but remember that most teenagers are secretive and this has to be respected as part of their growing up. So don't suspect them unnecessarily. There are several societies which give information and advice to parents.

Habit disorders can be exasperating and worrying for parents. Some of these seem to reach a peak at 10 or 11 years and die away in time. There may be twitching, sniffing, grunting, excessive nail biting, sucking fingers, lips or even biting fingers. There may be serious sleep difficulties and night terrors. Stammering may become noticeable, especially when the child is anxious or excited.

Some children develop food fads. We all have these in a moderate way but it may be a pointer if this is excessive. Some children are the opposite: they eat indiscriminately. (I recall one unhappy fat boy who was never at ease unless he could feel his bag of sweets safely in his pocket and he ate them whenever he was distressed.) More alarming is the adolescent, usually a girl, who refuses to eat, is very thin, and may be suffering from anorexia nervosa. This requires urgent help.

Other children may develop vague aches and pains, feel ill and even vomit on Monday mornings in their fear of school or of leaving home.

What to do
In general, the less you worry and the more you can relax the quicker the symptoms will pass. Extra loving, opportunities for success and self-esteem, a break to give a breathing space will often do the trick. But if you think the signs have been going on too long, or are so intense that they disrupt your and the child's happiness, don't hesitate to seek help. Consult your health visitor, the family doctor, the head teacher, or ask for a referral to the school psychological service. Don't waste time and energy feeling guilty, and don't let the child be overwhelmed with guilt. There will be many reasons and it is unlikely to be all your or the child's fault.

3
Self-help relaxation

There are inevitably some events that are so severely stressful that no child should be expected to cope with them alone. Frequent physical or mental abuse, rejection, too many life changes, long periods of pain or disturbing hospital experience can only be helped by loving and caring support by adults. However, everyday anxieties and tensions will not be disturbing if the child learns to use relaxation and quieting techniques to cope without being distressed.

We have seen that the effects of stress are not caused by the situation itself but by the child's reaction to it, and parents and teachers usually know better than any expert the kind of events which produce tension in individual children. By learning to recognise tension and substitute a relaxation response instead, children can discover their own ways of coping with stress. It can be very heartening to a frightened child to know that the horrid feelings of fear and its accompanying inexplicable physical effects can be lessened or prevented without adult help. Children gradually learn how much keying up they can take and make adjustments for themselves. There are of course some fearful situations which call for vigorous action rather than relaxation. A child must be encouraged to yell loudly and struggle to escape if there is danger of sexual assault. But after a fright, the long-term emotional effects can be minimised by using relaxation techniques to shut off the repeated recall of alarming events rather than dwelling on them (and this applies to adults too).

There are many advantages in learning how to relax at an early age. Young pre-school children relax naturally and we could learn a lot from them, but the ability gets lost as they grow older. By learning relaxation in a fun way at home and later at school as part of physical education and other subjects, children can acquire the techniques before they are cluttered up with tension and anxiety. They learn it as a physical skill at the age when this is easy and interesting because mastering physical skills is of paramount importance in childhood. There is also an advantage in using a self-help method: it is under the child's own control and once it is learnt it can often be used without anyone noticing. This is particularly useful in stressful situations in school or for older children in social situations.

How can relaxing muscles calm the mind?

There is now plenty of evidence to show that when muscles are voluntarily relaxed, mental turmoil dies down. It is not possible to be very agitated and relaxed at the same time. Notice the word 'voluntarily' though, because the effect is not the same when muscles are relaxed by drugs.

The reason seems to be this: just as the first reaction to threat is muscle tension (we often say 'It made me jump' when we are frightened) and the message is passed to the brain to prepare for action, so when the muscles are relaxed the message received is that all is well and there is no need to stir up the body to fight. Tension is the 'get the body worked up' signal; relaxation is the opposite: the 'quieten down, no need to be alarmed' signal.

There is considerable research evidence to support this theory. In 1979 the first International Conference on Stress and Tension control was held in London, and there have been annual meetings in different countries since then. Research papers presented from many parts of the world give impressive evidence of the success of relaxation training in the field of medicine, dentistry, and psychiatry as well as in athletics. There are also advances in its use in education: relaxation has been found to be successful with over-active and disruptive children in the classroom, and from Sweden comes a comprehensive research report on the effects of teaching relaxation in schools; the results were sufficiently conclusive for the authorities to introduce relaxation as part of the curriculum in all physical education programmes. Other countries are now introducing relaxation into schools and there have been reports on the beneficial effects on learning, health and behaviour of the children.

The many research reports all present a similar message: stress *can* be controlled, excessive stress *can* be reduced and relaxation techniques *can* be learnt by children.

What relaxation training involves

Recognising tension
Learning to relax will involve becoming aware of the difference between muscle tension and relaxation. Many people are not conscious of holding muscles tight and tense, so the training will involve various methods for assessing degrees of muscle tension and relaxation.

Applying relaxation to everyday situations
The next step is to recognise unnecessary muscle tension in daily living situations and to learn how to release it.

A 'calm down' technique
This is very useful in an emergency, involving quick selective muscle

relaxation accompanied by calm breathing. Its advantage is that it can be done anywhere without anyone noticing and only takes a few minutes.

Brief 'time out' relaxation
This is done sitting in a chair, even a hard work chair, and involves relaxation of most of the body for five minutes or so. It is a short period of respite and gives feelings of refreshment and calm in the middle of work pressures.

Full deep relaxation
This requires the body to be fully supported and each part is relaxed in turn. Breathing is calm, and after a period of undisturbed quiet the body becomes fully rested, the mind idles gently and the mental churning dies down.

'Thought stopping' or 'quieting'
This involves switching the attention to a neutral or pleasant thought or sound. Only very simple techniques are discussed in this book; some meditative techniques can be misused and young people may withdraw inwardly for long periods and become dissociated unless they are carefully guided.

Physical activity
Tension is energy held back, and pleasurable physical activity will discharge some of this tension.

As children grow older they will probably wish to add other techniques, so a variety of methods is described later.

When to use relaxation

To cope with stress
There is a close relationship between emotional states and muscle tension. Mental tension dies down when muscles are voluntarily relaxed.

To relieve fatigue and avoid the aches and pains
When muscles are held tight for long periods they may go into cramp-like spasm causing discomfort and pain. Energy is unnecessarily used up in tension. Relaxation not only postpones the onset of fatigue but enables a quicker recovery after effort.

Use it to cope with pain
Relaxation helps ordinary pain to hurt less, while tension increases it. Children receiving treatment at the doctor's or dentist will find that simple relaxation and calm breathing helps diminish pain.

To improve performance of physical skills

Unnecessary tension impedes good movement and body use. Relaxation is used by dancers, athletes, musicians, and actors to produce effortless grace, and ease and full efficiency of movement.

To aid mental preparation for competitive events

Many top class athletes use relaxation as an aid to mental warming up before an event so that they are mentally and emotionally prepared. It is used with visualisation techniques to help them concentrate on the factors necessary for good performance and to shut off any distractions.

To improve relationships with others

Children easily make friends with someone who is relaxed and at ease, but react against one who is unable to show warmth and responsiveness. Relaxation can help the child to be more at ease.

To aid study and creative thinking

Research has shown that relaxation and simple meditation techniques can enhance learning and help mind clearing, leaving it uncluttered for clear thinking when doing complicated creative work.

To improve other methods of mind quieting

Meditation, autogenic training, yoga, biofeedback are all enhanced by learning muscle relaxation first.

Learning to relax in school

Learning together in a group, sharing experiences and discussing how the techniques can be applied produces excellent results. I have now seen many classes at work and am impressed by the way the children respond. They manifestly enjoy learning and the staff report that the benefits are obvious: the children are calmer, there has been less nailbiting, they go more quietly into the next lesson after physical education. Older children have used the techniques to help them to cope with exam nerves, before competitions, addressing school assembly and to alleviate minor health ailments, especially painful menstrual periods and headaches. Some have used relaxation successfully to cope with insomnia especially at times of stress.

4

The role of parents and teachers

Fear, anxiety and tension are catching. When we are with someone who is on edge or frightened we soon begin to feel upset or apprehensive too. But relaxation is as contagious as tension and a calm voice and relaxed manner helps those around to calm down also. Children are watchers, listeners, observers and are greedy for clues about the real feelings of adults. They pick up signals of tension, irritation and anger even when parents think they are disguising this. So relaxation is important for parents too.

To be a parent is to have a job which carries more responsibility and has more far-reaching effects than any other. It can be richly rewarding and fulfilling but incredibly demanding in the way it shapes the whole life of the adults concerned. It still remains the key industry of our society, yet it is a job for which there is little or no training, the hours are longer than industry would tolerate, it is poorly paid and there are usually no holidays away from the job. This will apply to whoever is taking on the main task of caring for the children, whether it is the woman or the man.

Mothers have in addition biological stresses that no man has to meet. Mixed up with the joy of having a child, there can be fatigue of a kind never experienced before. Part of this is due to the drop in hormone levels after childbirth but in addition the menstrual cycle will affect her feelings. Most women experience fluctuating moods and extra fatigue when hormone levels change. The majority of mothers cope without much difficulty and indeed some women experience a surge of creativity and liveliness at these times, but there are some who know only too well the pre-menstrual tension which can erupt irrationally and affect the whole family. Once the flare-up has subsided and feelings have settled down to normal, she may feel ashamed and guilty about her behaviour.

Until the children grow up and leave home it would be an unusual mother who, for many reasons, is not sometimes beset by feelings of guilt: it seems to be part of her role. She has to apportion her time and thought between her children and her partner; if she goes out to work she will feel guilty about leaving the children even though she may be bringing them new interests from outside; if she remains at home to enjoy her children and look after the house there will be social and financial pressures to make her feel she should be at work; she may also feel it is her responsibility to look after ageing relatives.

If you are a mother, don't take the job so seriously that guilt takes over and makes you miss a lot of the fun and shared joy of children. I heard a wise family physician advise a mother to cut out the 'oughts' and 'shoulds' and substitute some 'let's do' instead.

Mothers need to relax

If you want your children to relax, begin with yourself. Take stock and rediscover the real you. Children want above all a mother who is happy, who shares in their interests, and seems to like them for what they are. If their basic emotional needs are met they will take any of your flare-ups in their stride. It is not being selfish to consider yourself sometimes and to keep up some of your interests. Being a parent inevitably involves putting the child's needs before your own, but it is rarely wise to make excessive sacrifices for the children. They may come to feel oppressively guilty later on, or be resentful if the sacrifices were inappropriate. It is important for you to be a person in your own right and not to be too tired to enjoy life with your partner. Decide on your priorities regarding housework, and ignore what you and your partner consider is not essential. Never mind what the neighbours think: an immaculate house always ready for the stray visitor simply doesn't fit in with creative lively children, and you must guard against your own fatigue. If you are managing single-handed you will need even more to make time to relax and keep fatigue in check.

You probably learnt some relaxation techniques for childbirth, but it is now that you need them even more than before. Try to practise at home, and let the children see you do it. It is even better if your partner joins in too because the stress of modern working life is paying a heavy toll on men in middle age and relaxation techniques are being increasingly recognised as a weapon against cardiovascular disease.

To see you both relaxing for brief spells will be an excellent example for the children. If you go out to work, when you get home have a short flopping spell of relaxing before you get on with the evening chores. Let the children join in with you when they are young and tell them why you are doing it. Even ten minutes of sitting really relaxed with your feet up will give you more energy afterwards. Let the children get used to the idea that this replenishing of energy is a sensible thing to do.

If your problem is depression, don't hesitate to seek help if this is really serious, but there are some self-help methods you can use. There is now evidence that exercise helps to lift the inexplicable feelings of sadness and gloom and it should then be followed by relaxation. So if you can, join a class for some pleasant exercise in good company: it will be well worth the effort. If this is not possible, choose some music you enjoy and do some exercises every day at home. Then after the activity, have a spell of deep relaxation. It is often useful to have a cassette recording to help you if you are on your own because when you are depressed or anxious a voice telling you what to do is encouraging and gives you some extra support (there is some information about cassettes at the end of the book). Never feel guilty about taking time off to exercise and relax because the whole family will gain in the end. The household simmers down when you are calm instead of tense and exhausted. I know it is easy to say this, and I am well aware of the great difficulties of relaxing if you have a hyperactive child, because you too catch these feelings of tension, but try to relax whenever you can.

Meeting physical needs

Nutrition

A healthy well-nourished child is more easily able to cope with stress, but parents are now being bombarded by conflicting views as to what constitutes good nutrition. Yesterday's 'good' foods have become today's baddies and there is increasing publicity about the ill-effects of pollution and chemical additives. However, most nutritionists agree that a good mixed diet with plenty of variety (including fresh vegetables, fruit and fibre) will give the normal child all that is required. There is no food magically 'good' in itself, and no food is absolutely necessary. Its value lies in what the body can make of it. A happy active child utilises food to the full, but one who is frightened and anxious cannot digest properly and may be malnourished however excellent and well-planned the diet may be. Happiness is a priority for good digestion so meals should be pleasant occasions with as few arguments or nagging about table manners as possible. For those suffering from nervous indigestion, and this might be parents as well as children, a few minutes relaxing before meals is a great help.

It is important for parents to be aware of the surprising quantities of hidden stimulants in the food and drink that children enjoy, but which all add to arousal and may result in tension, over-activity and fatigue. Tea, coffee, cocoa, chocolate all contain stimulants and the various Cola drinks have considerable amounts of caffeine in them. Parents of hyperactive children should avoid giving these in any quantity and to notice if the child reacts to chemical additives in foods. In particular the artificial colouring in some orange drinks and foods has been found to affect some over-active children. Most experts also advise against too much sugar. This surprisingly can soon cause a marked drop in blood sugar and has been found to be a culprit in migraine.

Exercise

Children have a natural urge for movement and vigorous activity is an outlet for surplus energy. The healthier the child, the more surplus energy he has over and above the normal requirements. Exercise frees the body of tension and anxiety and leads to relaxation. This is nature's way of using up the biochemicals of stress. Lively children denied opportunities for sufficient exercise become irritable and may explode into violent action.

In childhood, the acquisition of physical skills takes priority over everything else; it is the time for mastery over the body. Upon their ability to climb, jump, throw, kick a ball, do handstands, play games, will depend their acceptance by other children. A boy who is hopeless at games, who cannot kick a ball, is fearful of wrestling and who is always chosen last for teams will inevitably lose prestige throughout childhood and this may influence his feelings about himself even when he is an adult. Although as he gets older academic skills may be recognised and the efficiency in sport plays a lesser part, the damage may have been done and feelings of inadequacy remain for the rest of life.

Girls suffer less but many women will recall the indignities of being awkward and clumsy at school and how they dreaded physical education lessons.

Parents should do all they can to encourage a child to develop some skill in an enjoyable physical activity where some success is possible. There is such a wide choice of activities that even a mini success will boost self-esteem.

In addition to the effects on personality, exercise has many physical benefits. Vigorous physical activity is essential for the healthy growth of bones and muscle. During the years of childhood there is steady growth in the long bones and in muscular density. Activity, or lack of it, has a rapid effect on the level of calcium in the bones. According to Brian Cratty, author of *Perceptual and Motor Development in Infants and Children*, within one week of inactivity as much as half the calcium is lost in the bones. Exercise also affects the whole body, stimulating circulation and respiration so that all body cells are better nourished as a result and waste products more readily eliminated.

A habit of regular exercise will be of value throughout life. Experiments showed that elderly women who still took exercise did not lose calcium in their bones (a common factor in ageing), as much as those who were inactive did, and there is now plenty of evidence to show that sensible exercise in adult life can minimise the risks of cardiovascular disease. It is in childhood that the pattern of taking healthy enjoyable exercise is established and parents have a role in encouraging this.

The aim of a comprehensive exercise programme should be to develop the four 'S's –

Stamina
Suppleness
Strength
Satisfaction

In a natural environment children would be able to climb, clamber, swing and hang from a support, swim and acquire many skills in a spontaneous way. This is rarely possible in modern urban life and parents and teachers have to devise ways to give children opportunities with climbing apparatus, ball games, skipping, dance, swimming classes and to have a varied physical education programme in schools. Activities which can be enjoyed at home, or in which the whole family can join are an excellent introduction.

Swimming

Swimming is probably the best exercise for the whole body. It is also relaxing because it is not possible to swim if muscles are tense, it has survival value, and is probably the only activity in which all the family can join together, from grandparents down to the new baby. You can learn at any age, so if you missed out on this when you were young, have a go. I know a number of mothers who learnt when they were concerned about water safety for their young children, and also grandparents who learnt after they were sixty. It is never too late to learn and is fun for the whole family once you have got over the first embarrassments.

Dance

Dance is an emotional experience. All young children express their feelings with dance movements: they jump for joy, wriggle with embarrassment, stamp in anger, freeze motionless with terror. As we grow older we learn to deny ourselves these outward expressions of emotion. Dance provides not only a release of feelings but it gives opportunities for self-expression, imagination and it leads to grace and ease of movement. It is valuable for boys as well as girls and many schools include dance as part of physical education.

Stylised forms of dance such as disco, tap, musical comedy are generally out of place for the pre-pubertal child; the pseudo-adult posturings with sexually precocious hip movements are merely mini replicas of adult dance. They are not only inappropriate for young children, though it amuses grown-ups to watch, but they deprive children of the imaginative body-mind experience that expressive free dance can give. (Some ideas for introducing dance to children are given in the chapter on techniques, and some of these activities can be fun to use as party games.)

Older children will be ready for their own form of social dance, and however much we may disapprove of the over-excitement of loud music and flashing lights, we must recognise that this is the dance of today, it often involves a good range of inventive movement, and it forms the foundation for social contacts with the other sex.

Posture

Many adults suffer from the effects of faulty postural habits which originated in inappropriate tensions in childhood. Backache, neck pain, lack of mobility in the spine are the more obvious results, but many other disorders are caused by continued faulty use of the body. Poor posture caused by inappropriate tension puts a strain on the muscles and joints and increases the general wear and tear on the body.

Posture also influences how other people unconsciously assess the personality of a young person. A slouching drooping posture signals messages of slovenliness, depression, or uncertainty; an over stiff posture gives a picture of nervous tension and lack of warmth. An easy upright posture, with a good head position, inspires confidence in others and also produces feelings of inner calm.

Look out for bad posture in children before it becomes a habit. It is the continual misuse that is the problem and causes the body to protest; movement aids relaxation but if muscles are held contracted in a faulty way for long periods the whole body will be distorted. Notice whether your child sits hunched over homework, holds the pen tightly; whether the head is usually poked forward or tilted to one side (these compress the spine at the neck). Be aware of a round back and notice if children always carry their school bags on one side and look out for one shoulder habitually held higher than the other because this is the first sign of a lateral curve in the spine. Let them see these faults in a mirror . . . it will save you some nagging if they discover it for themselves. Bad posture usually originates from a faulty head position and the Alexander Technique, used by many famous people, pays great attention to the correct posture of the head and good body use. It emphasises the lengthened spine, the expanded body and the feeling of 'forward and up'.

You can help by seeing that at meals or when studying the child sits well back on the chair so that the thighs are well supported, and that the chair is drawn up close to the table. In this way there is no room to slouch and good posture is more likely.

Meeting the emotional needs of children

All children have basic emotional needs which must be satisfied if they are to be happy, confident and use their abilities to the full. Parents carry most of the responsibility for fulfilling these requirements, but teachers also play an important part. It is inevitable that at times these needs cannot be met, however caring and loving parents and teachers may be. If you decide that one of these needs is not being satisfied try to help by boosting up the others.

The need for love and security
Like 'stress', 'love' is another word that has many different meanings and is gloriously inexplicable. Children need one person to 'love' them beyond all reason. This involves acceptance, affection and, above all, respect. For children to flourish they must not only be able to receive love, but to have opportunities to give it also; on this will depend the quality of their later relationships. It is sad that children most in need of being loved are usually so unlovable and find it hard to show any affection. It is difficult to feel warmly towards a child who is openly

rejecting, shows no affection, shies away from any caresses and gives none in return. These hurt children are unrewarding for parents and teachers because we all need some feedback to make us respond warmly, yet rejection is the hell they fear. They desperately need the unconditional love and approval of someone, even if it cannot be the parent.

As well as being respected, children need their quota of physical contact: stroking, cuddling, hugging, even rough and tumbling wrestling with adults or their friends. (One 8-year-old when asked what 'secret happy picture' he used in visualising during relaxation said that it was 'wrestling and fighting with my best friend'.)

A feeling of being loved gives children security, but in addition they require a sense of order, routine, reasonable discipline and some predictability about what is going to happen to them. We have seen that changes in lifestyle are stressful and children need a safe framework of stability without too many changes. If major changes are inevitable, it helps to prepare the child for these well in advance.

Recognition and praise

A pre-requisite for coping is a healthy self-regard. It is from other people that we discover our worth. Praise is essential for the development of a happy child, and it is perhaps even more important to give praise for endeavour than for achievement. There is something somewhere in every child that is praiseworthy and its recognition will give the self-respect so necessary for future development. The best insulator against stress is self-esteem. As they grow older children will look to their peers for recognition and the opinion of friends will often be more important than those of parents or teachers.

School, with its emphasis on competition rather than cooperation, with exams and tests of individual excellence, is inevitably a source of loss of self-respect, especially for the less academic child or the one hopeless at games. However, when children feel secure and their other needs are met, they can take occasional failure in their stride and even learn to gain from it.

New experience and responsibility

This may appear to conflict with the need for security, but people desire both the fat of security and the pepper of insecurity. Children are hungry for new experiences and adventure and these contribute towards their mental growth. They need to try themselves out physically and intellectually and learn to take responsibility. Over-protected children are stifled and will be fearful of taking responsibility. Like all skills it requires practice and we should give children unobtrusive guidance without breathing down their necks all the time. In adolescence the guidance gradually lessens as they become capable of more and more responsibility if they are trusted and given opportunities.

Creative hobbies

To be creative is to be flexible and relaxed enough to be original, inventive and to produce something that is specially your own, and it becomes a rewarding experience. A hobby of any kind is a buffer against stress and it is in childhood these interests are encouraged. An absorbing hobby cuts off intruding unpleasant thoughts and helps in coping with stress. As children grow older, when studying may take up much of their spare time, they will find it difficult to keep up these interests. It is worth while for them to make every effort to set aside time for an absorbing pursuit because it will help students to have a mental rest, will enhance study afterwards and prove invaluable in later life

Parents also have emotional needs

Your own self-esteem will be shaky at times and you will rarely receive the praise you deserve. The humdrum household chores of cleaning, cooking, washing and ironing, taking and fetching the children from school and clubs, do not call for acclaim, and unless your partner looks for occasions when praise can be given you will be short on this emotional support. Parents are likely to be particularly deflated when children reach adolescence and criticise your home, your lifestyle, your clothes, even your moral attitudes, and appear to be wilfully disobedient. This is hard to take, but is part of their growing up and you can mark it as a step forward. It will pass if you praise whenever you can, show some respect, and don't get too worked up at your own hurt. Laughter is a marvellous relaxer and a light humorous touch works wonders to diffuse an explosive situation. There is tremendous fun in sharing the strong enthusiasms of young people even if they are maddening at times.

'NOWS' or 'MINI MAGIC MOMENTS'

Help your children to cultivate the recognition of special moments of delight, to say 'This is a NOW' or 'This is MMM'. These are not major events but the kind of delights which give a feeling of happiness: the first barefoot running on sand, a picnic meal when they are hungry, the arrival of a friend, the first signs of spring, a surprising 'A' for an essay . . . there are many events which would easily be forgotten but which if registered can be recalled later. This is especially useful for children who are apt to moan and whine, but it is useful for adults too.

5

Techniques of relaxation

General introduction

The aim of these techniques is to introduce children and young adults to the skill of muscle relaxation and mental quieting which will help them to take responsibility for their own feelings of well-being and confidence and develop strategies for coping with stress. In the early years the exercises are meant to be fun and to be vigorous enough to release bottled-up feelings of frustration in an acceptable way. Because the two behaviours of muscle tension and relaxation cannot happen together, children are shown how to become aware of the contrast between tension and relaxation of muscles. They can then learn simple methods of calming down. As they grow older they will learn how to apply the techniques in everyday life.

Techniques will have to be selected and adapted according to the needs of different children. In planning and teaching the exercises I have borne in mind the typical characteristics of children in each age group and it will be helpful for parents and teachers to be aware of these, so I have introduced each section of techniques with a 'profile' of a child in this age range. However, although all children pass through the same stages of development, they do so at different rates – when they are surging through one stage of physical, intellectual or emotional development they may be marking time in another – so the profiles are therefore only a rough guide to common characteristics and your child may well not match the profile in every way.

In general, until the age of puberty, girls are up to two years ahead of boys in growth and intellectual development. They talk more fluently, read more easily and are generally ahead on school work. So don't think your boy is backward because the girls are ahead in the early school years. It is exasperating for the boys, but they do usually catch up later.

Profile: Early school years

5-year-olds

These children are still fairly chubby, about to lose their first teeth and still have some baby ways. They are home centred and usually eager to please adults. They are often preoccupied with improving their physical abilities: they run, jump, dance spontaneously, can almost skip and constantly seek approval for their mastery over bodily skills with 'Look at me', 'Watch me do this', and seem hungry for approval. They give an impression of completeness in posture and natural grace, but their control over fine muscles has not yet matured and intricate activities are often inappropriate. They are rarely ready for the coordination of eye and hand that is required in catching and hitting a small ball. Boys are from the start better at throwing than girls: even before birth they have developed relatively longer forearms and have a different set to their shoulders from girls who throw with a characteristic round arm movement.

5-year-olds play in pairs and may have a 'best friend' or sometimes an imaginary friend who takes the blame for misdemeanours. They are not cooperative in groups, though, and play in the presence of, rather than with, other children. They like routine and dislike change, often choosing to be read the same story over and over again and insisting on a set bedtime routine.

Many well-prepared children are delighted to start school, but others may be frozen with fear. There is a change in routine, new rules, a noisy playground, older teasing children, strange lavatories (some children are so scared of these that they avoid using them and may wet in class or hang on until they get home and have to rush to the toilet).

At first these children may be mentally exhausted when they get home and become irritable and troublesome, so don't be surprised. It passes as they get used to school so it can be regarded as a temporary setback which requires extra understanding. This sometimes accounts for an increase in thumb sucking, nose picking and sniffing at this time. These, too, will pass, but it is a good time for some fun relaxation sessions to relieve their tension and frustration.

Their fears are usually specific – of dogs, cats, burglars, older children, thunder (though this fear is often picked up from the reactions of adults).

Illness in itself is stressful and children starting school are likely to pick up the usual childhood infections.

This is a time when many have nightmares. Soothing massage and some relaxation will be helpful.

6- and 7-year-olds

This is the gappy tooth age when children are eager to learn and to make friends and are usually a delight for the teacher. They relish physical activities like climbing, they can hang by the knees and turn somersaults, enjoy gymnastics and dancing, can skip with a rope, and begin to use a bat successfully. If they are allowed to go barefoot whenever possible they will enjoy the freedom and develop well-formed feet.

They will often be argumentative and quarrelsome with their play-mates with many complaints of 'It's not fair', 'I shan't play'. If it seems that your children argue from morning to night, take heart. Most children of this age do this and they are actually learning something: just how much people will tolerate, and how far they can go without retaliation. Their fears become more imaginative – ghosts, witches (perhaps this is why they enjoy the 'wicked witch' activity), shadows on the wall.

Their delight in acquiring physical skills makes this a good time to teach relaxation techniques in a fun way. The techniques they specially enjoy are stamping, punching, robots, and wicked witch exercises which help to release tension and frustration, but these should always be followed by quiet controlled exercises so that they experience the contrast of self-induced calm.

Introducing the techniques

Begin by asking the children to remember what they feel like when they are lonely, frightened or angry (one child said after a tantrum that he felt as if lots of big fingers were clawing at his inside). Most will say they feel tight and horrid inside and outside. Then let them know that there are some ways in which, all by themselves, they can help to make the unpleasant feelings gradually go away.

To do this they must first be able to recognise the difference between tense muscles and relaxed ones. This should be introduced in an enjoyable way through the contrasts of vigorous strong movements involving tension to release bottled-up feelings, followed by smooth quiet movements leading to stillness and calm. At first use words they recognise, like 'This is stiff', 'This is floppy', but later use the words 'tense' and 'relaxed' so that they will soon be able to respond immediately to the word 'relax'. Then always follow this with a short spell of full relaxation lying on the floor. Initially this will be for no more than half a minute, but can be increased later if they are not fidgety. Ask them to become aware of the pleasant feeling of calm they have produced for themselves.

Parents and teachers will be able to decide on the best way of introducing techniques and selecting them, but the following are some activities which have been used successfully with children of this age group at home and at school.

How to organise a session

At home (for 4- to 7-year-olds)
Move the furniture a little so that there is some room for movement. Join in when you can, or invite one other child to take part in the fun. Each session should be no longer than 7 to 10 minutes at first, but when the children are familiar with the ideas it can be longer. Choose two of the activities suggested in the techniques section and always end with a short spell of full relaxation (half a minute at first, but increase this time later).

Examples

First session

1 'Ogres' – the stamping, energy releasing activity followed by quiet creeping and standing still (see p. 44).
2 'The Wicked Witch' (see p. 48) – add your own variations after a while or let the children suggest ideas. Follow this with shaking loose and a dance for joy.
3 Relaxation lying on the floor (see p. 66) – talk them through this at first so that they don't feel strange. In the beginning allow about half a minute of quiet, then increase this later, when the children feel comfortable relaxing.

Later sessions

Gradually progress to other activities, but take care not to hurry the children. All children enjoy repetition and feel secure when they know what is coming.
1 'Crosspatch and floppy puppet' (see p. 46).
2 'Robot and floating feather' (see p. 50).
3 Relaxation followed by 'my secret happy picture' visualisation (see p. 68).

These are only suggestions; choose the techniques you think your children will enjoy and invent some of your own. Use music or percussion (even a spoon and a saucepan lid is effective) if you think it helps. Children enjoy some of the techniques as party games. In general, the activities described in the techniques section are progressive, but you can pick and choose according to the ability of the children.

Visualisation

Many young children have a remarkable eidetic memory – the ability to reproduce an almost photographic mental image of something they have previously seen. Often they can recall an image with uncanny detail. It is believed that most young children have this ability, but it disappears as they grow older. It seems therefore a good time to introduce some visualisation techniques as an added calming method. Let them choose their own special 'secret happy picture' to use while they are relaxing. It could be a place they love to be in, a pet, a treasured toy, a well loved person . . . it is their own choice. Don't tell them what to visualise because your 'picture' might be quite unsuitable. And don't ask them to divulge their secret, however tempted you may be. It is best to introduce this after they have learnt a little about relaxation. Not all children can manage this kind of visualisation, so drop the idea if it seems unsuitable.

Help them to apply relaxation techniques

Once children have learnt some of the techniques, give them ideas for occasions when they can use these calming methods, for example: visiting the dentist or hospital, having a cut knee dressed, going to a new school, whenever they want to feel brave, when they are angry or frustrated or to calm down after a temper tantrum, or when they are frightened at night. A relaxation cassette recording made for children may be helpful before they go to sleep at night or on a long car journey when the children are restless.

In school (all ages)

Either end each physical education lesson with a spell of relaxation, or make the techniques a basis for the whole lesson. Don't progress too quickly; let the children enjoy some repetition of the activities, introducing their or your own variations. Follow these activities with full relaxation on the floor. Remember that children lose heat quickly so the relaxation session cannot be for long in a cold hall. But even a very short spell can be surprisingly effective. You can use some of the techniques in the classroom. The finger tension and relaxation is particularly suitable as well as a brief 'Time out' relaxation in their chairs.

Older children will enjoy a longer period of full relaxation and visualisation, and sometimes let them test a partner (or you) for relaxation of arms and legs.

Discuss ways in which relaxation can be used in everyday situations.

The techniques – early school years

OGRES

Objectives

To release feelings of frustration in an enjoyable vigorous activity. To experience the difference between being tense and being relaxed. To introduce ideas of self-help relaxation and to share the activities with a friend (though it can be equally enjoyable for an individual child). (Although this is useful at any time, it can be helpful after a tantrum or when one is building up. It helps timid children who are afraid to let out their feelings.)

1 Stand up and clench your fists and try to feel cross. Now stamp your feet hard on the ground, like an angry ogre. Then move all round the room stamping hard as you go. Lift your knees high as you stamp.
2 STOP. Stand very still and quiet and listen.

3 Now you are escaping from the ogre. Walk very softly round the room, so quietly that no one can hear you. Move softly, smoothly, without making a sound. No one can hear you. Go slower and slower until it is safe to stop.

4 Stand very still, tall and easy, and notice how quiet and calm you feel now.

Working with groups

This can be fun as a party game or as part of a physical education lesson at school. The stamping should be quite fast. Use a sharp brisk voice for the stamping and a quieter lingering one for the silent walking. Let them hold the still position long enough to appreciate the difference in feeling. Progress to the next exercise as soon as they have managed this one.

   Musical accompaniment adds to the enjoyment. Improvising on the piano is fine if you are able. Percussion with drum, tambourine, saucepan and spoon can easily be done, sharp taps for stamping, stroking for quiet walking.

CROSSPATCH
FLOPPY PUPPET

Crosspatch

1 Stand with your feet apart, clench your fists tight and feel cross. Now punch hard in front of you, first with one hand and then the other . . . punch and punch and punch. Now punch all over the place, sideways, upwards and in front.
2 Now join this up with the stamping exercise so that you stamp round the room and punch at the same time . . . stamping and thumping about. Make a cross face as you do this if you can.
3 STOP! Stand quite still. Feel how you have stamped the cross feelings away.

Objectives
A progression from the Ogre exercise, introducing more body movement. To introduce contrasts of tension and relaxation.

Floppy Puppet

1 Now do the opposite. Make yourself into a floppy puppet. Go all loose with your arms floppy, your head floppy, your hands loose . . . all silly and floppy and limp.

2 Move round the room, flippity flop. Go slower and slower until you fall down all in a heap.

3 Stay relaxed and still like this. Don't move. Notice how quiet you feel now.

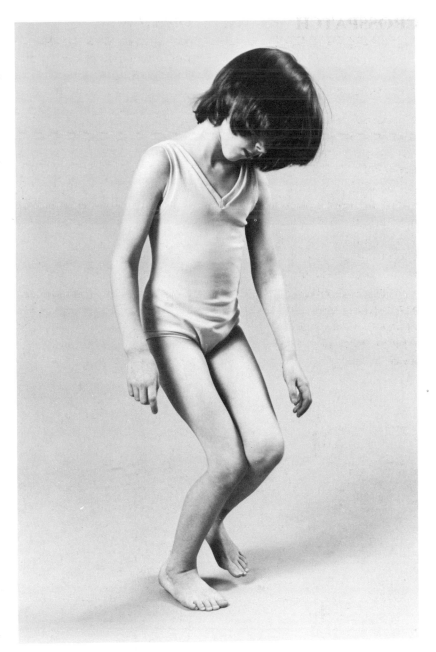

Working with groups

Don't be afraid that this will make the children aggressive. It can do the opposite by releasing their bottled-up feelings in a safe and fun way. This works well with a group and a progression could be with one group of children stamping and punching while the others wait. Then the other half answer with relaxed floppy movements. Draw attention to the different feelings of tension and relaxation.

Musical accompaniment should be of two kinds, one with a marked beat, the other more flowing and gradually slowing down to a stop.

THE WICKED WITCH

Objectives

To introduce tension in strong twisted positions in a way to stir the imagination.

To foster artistic expression in movement.

To use as a party game or with groups of children.

To introduce methods of shaking muscles loose.

(Select someone to be the witch, the parent, teacher or one of the children.)

1 Skip round the room. STOP! The witch has cast a spell on you and you are turned into a twisty stiff statue. Stay quite still, your fingers are stiff and spiky and you are all twisted and hard all over.

2 OFF! The spell is off and you can skip happily round the room. Think out a new twisty statue position. It can be high or low.

3 STOP! Stay quite still in your new twisty position. Feel hard and strong.

(Repeat several times.)

4 The witch has gone away so stand and shake all the tightness away. Shake yourself all over so that you wriggle and wobble. Shake your arms, your tummy, your head. Shake the spell away, then dance with joy.

5 Stand quite still with your arms relaxed and loose by your sides. It all feels lovely and calm and quiet.

Working with groups

This can be fun as a party game or at school. You can use music for the skipping and turn it off for the spell, sometimes, instead of having a person as the witch. Encourage a variety of twisted positions, high, low, narrow, wide. This can lead to some interesting paintings and written work by the older children. The general shaking is a whole body movement and is sometimes useful on its own to induce relaxation after tension or anxiety.

ROBOTS
FLOATING FEATHERS

Objectives
To introduce expressive movement in dramatic form.
To let the children experience contrasts of sudden jerky movements and free-flowing ones, and to help them become aware of the differing sensations of being stiff and being relaxed and controlled.

Working in groups
Children enjoy this activity in groups and will have plenty of ideas for the robots. Electronic music makes a good accompaniment. The floating free movements are more difficult and may need some help from adults. Arms should be loose and move smoothly, sometimes high, then low, and sometimes leading the body into turning movements.

   Give a few moments of stillness and quiet at the end so that they can appreciate the contrasts.

Robots

1 Stand up and become like a robot made of metal. Make yourself very stiff with your arms by your sides and your fingers straight.
2 Now move round the room. You can only move stiffly and in jerks. Your legs are stiff, your ankles bent up, your arms are jerky and bend sharply, your head moves suddenly and your muscles are tense and hard.
3 Stop in an awkward stiff position. It will look rather comic.

Floating Feathers

1 Now do the opposite – move smoothly and softly as if you were floating. Your arms are loose and easy and they help you to glide round freely and gently.

2 Gradually slow down and then settle down on the ground, still and relaxed.

3 Stay like that for a moment and notice what it feels like. Feel how different it is from the strong tight robot.

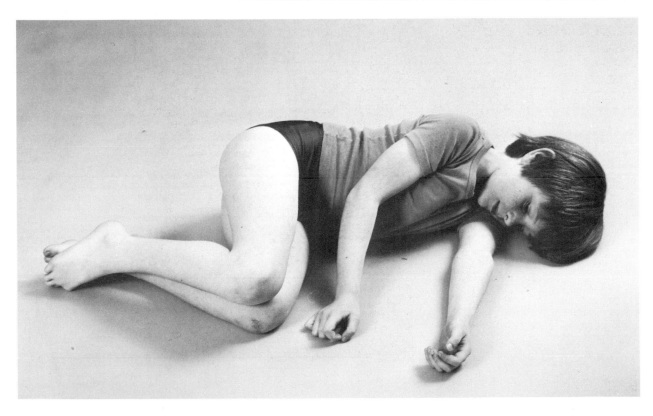

MAKE ME LAUGH

The clown

1 Become a clown and make the audience laugh. Do anything funny – fall over, make funny faces, jump about, look silly – anything you can think of to make people laugh.

Objectives

To release tension through laughter and to show that control can be quickly regained after unrestrained activity.

To help children who are shy or awkward and to give opportunities for 'show offs' and over-active children.

Working with groups

This has many possibilities for parties at home or for groups at school; equally individual children will enjoy acting these out for their parents. In a group, several children can be the clowns while the others are the audience. It is very important that after the riotous act the children should be shown how quickly they can regain control in the quiet restrained balancing act. The audience must be absolutely silent during this part of the performance to avoid disturbing the tight-rope walker.

Laughter of this kind is a fine releaser of tension.

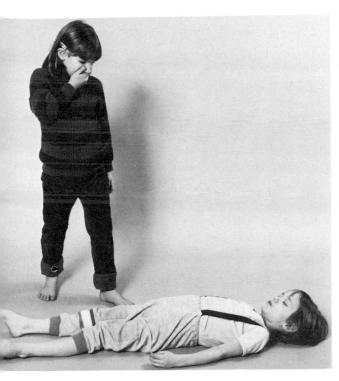

2 Suddenly fall down and lie still,
looking like a corpse. Then jump up
again and surprise everyone. Do it all
over again with some other ideas.

The tight-rope walker

1 Now become a tight-rope walker;
this is quite different – you have to be
very steady and calm for this or you
will fall off. Pretend there is a line on
the ground which is the tight-rope
very high up. You have to be very
steady as you walk along, very
controlled without even a wobble.
2 At the end, stand very still then give a
slow bow and a smile to the audience.

GROWING PLANT

Objectives
To help children discover varying degrees of tension.
To introduce sustained movements and body awareness.
To encourage imaginative dance and cooperation with a group.

1 Begin crouched on the floor with your hands just above your head. Let your fingers touch and point up like the shoot of a plant.
2 Begin to grow up with the tips of your fingers leading the way. They have to be strong so that they can break through the soil.
3 Now you grow taller and stronger, reaching as high as you possibly can.

4 The flower is beginning to open so gradually open your arms and turn your face upwards.

5 The wind blows so the plant sways and moves from side to side, and then forwards and backwards.

6 The plant gradually droops, beginning with your fingers, then your head, your body bends sideways or forwards until you collapse on the floor all loose and relaxed. Stay there very still.

(Check on the complete relaxation at the end. Fingers should be curled and very limp.)

Working with groups

Children can choose to be different plants, whatever their imaginations produce. Or groups of five can choose to be the same plants and contrast with other groups being different plants. Some children can become the breeze or stormy wind, influencing the movement of the plants.
A progression would be sharp sudden movements as the seeds scatter.

HIDE IT
(OR TIGHT FISTS)

Objective
To experience strong tension in hands and the contrast of limp wrists and fingers in a contest between a parent or friend.

1 Hide something small in your hand. Clench your fist as hard as you can and try not to let me open it. (Parent or friend tries to open it.) That is very tense.

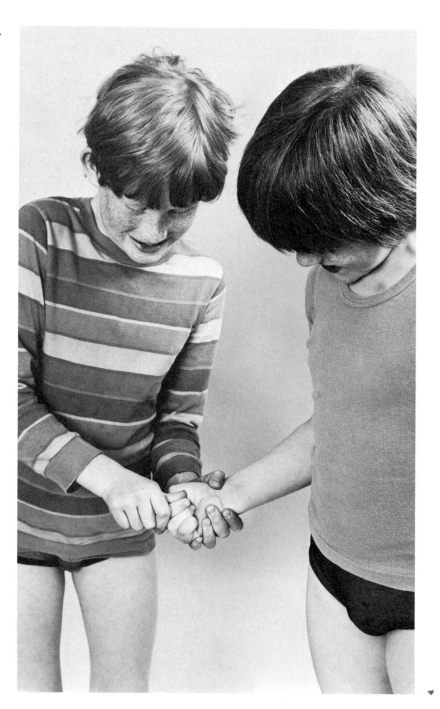

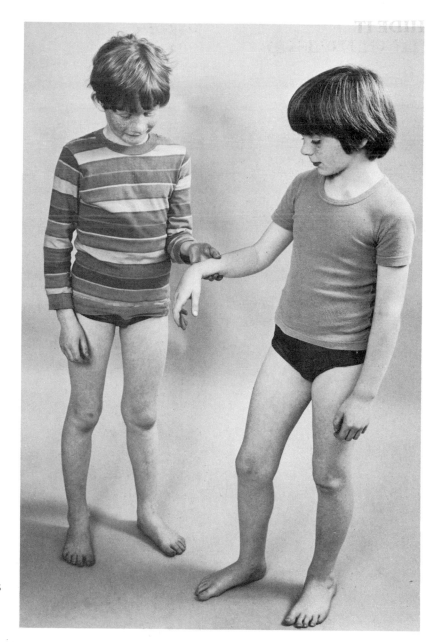

2 Now do the opposite – make your hand very loose and floppy. (Parent or partner shakes wrist so that hands are loose and floppy.) That is very relaxed.

3 Now do the same to me. (Child tries to open parent's hand then shakes it loose.)

Notes
Older children have fun trying this with a partner, and when they are good at it, in threes with a partner at each hand. See that each hand is tested.

This technique is sometimes useful for a child who holds the pen too tightly and some writing should follow immediately after this or the previous exercises.

READY TO FIGHT
FLOPPY ARMS

Objectives
Strong tension in arms and shoulders followed by relaxation of arms.
To become aware of the feelings of anger and tension and the contrast of relaxation.

1 Put your feet apart, tighten your shoulders and hands as if you were just going to fight. Notice how this makes you feel cross and tight all over.

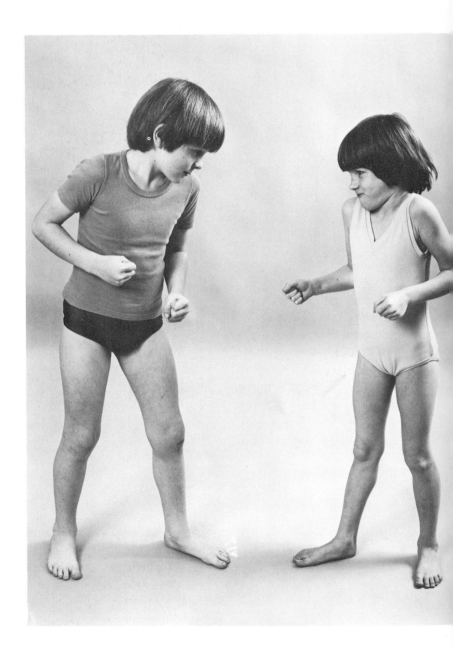

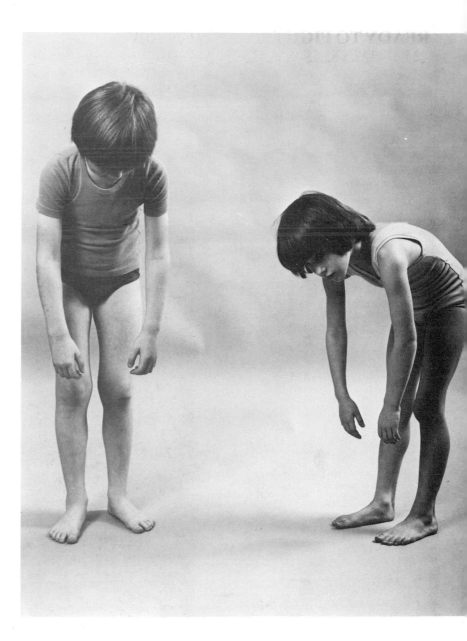

2 Lean forward and let your arms dangle loosely. Move your body a little and let your limp arms sway.
3 Then stand up, quite still, with your arms relaxed by your sides and feel the difference.

Working in groups
One half of the class make threatening tense movements, changing from one position to another; the other half respond with soft relaxed movements, weaving around the others trying to influence them to relax. Suitable music or percussion will add to the drama.

FIGHTING FINGERS
FLOATING FINGERS

Objectives
To combine with the previous exercise to release tension in the fingers.
To use as a quick method of quietening fidgety children.

1 Hold your hands in front of you so that the palms are facing each other. Stretch out your fingers as wide as you can so that they are really strong and stiff.
2 Now, make your fingers fight each other, scrabbling about, all the fingers working hard in the fight.

3 Now, let your fingers float loosely and gently round each other, like fish swimming lazily in and out.
4 Then let your hands hang down by your sides and feel what it is like when they are relaxed. It makes them feel heavy and warm.

Working in groups

Add other finger activities, pointing, bending, stretching, then move on to dance activities.
One partner can mirror the activities of the other, trying to match exactly.

Note

A famous children's hospital encourages the children to place a 'magic finger' on a painful spot to make it feel better.

TIGHT HANDS SHIVERY SHAKE

Objective
To help children recognise unnecessary tension in fingers when writing and learn how to release this.

Do your fingers look like this when you are writing? They are very tense and it can spoil your writing and make your hands tired.

1 Stretch out your fingers as far as they will go.

2 Then clench your fists tightly so that your knuckles look white. These movements are very tense.

3 Let your hands relax and shake them loosely all over the place: in front, up high, at your sides. Keep shaking them until they feel really loose.

4 When you hold your pen make sure you are not holding it too tightly.

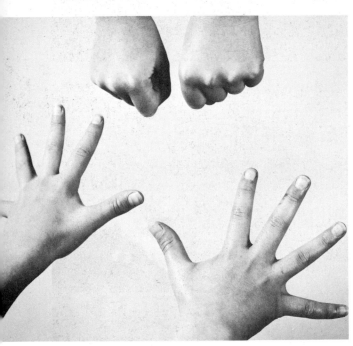

Working with groups

Use these techniques when children are restless in class, ending with relaxed hands resting on the desk or on the lap.

Use this before a recorder music session or before intricate craft work.

FUNNY FACES

To help children recognise how their feelings are reflected in their facial expressions, and that a happy pleasant face will not only make them feel better but will also have an influence on other people.

1 Angry face – make a very cross face. How does this make you feel? It often makes those around you feel horrid.
2 Fierce face – look very fierce or frightened. Open your mouth wide, raise your eyebrows, you can yell or roar if you like.
3 Sad face – make your face sad, as if you were just going to cry. Perhaps just doing this makes you feel sad.

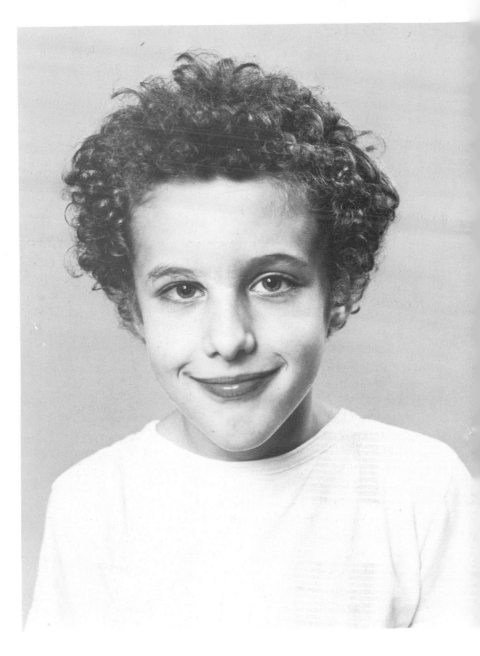

4 Happy face – now do the opposite; make a happy smiling face, the sort that other people like when they see you. Notice how this makes you feel.

Working with groups

This is fun when partners work together, one making a cross or fierce face and the other trying to respond with a smiling one.

One child makes a cross, fierce or sad face and the other tries to guess which it is and the sort of situation might cause this.

In bigger groups one half advance looking fierce and the other half respond with peaceful welcoming movements and smiling faces.

Children may discover how closely their facial expression relates to how they feel and that by changing a sad or cross face for a happier one often makes them feel better.

BODY FLOP

Objectives
To use the previous exercises to develop an understanding of full body relaxation. To provide a technique which can be used to quell anxiety, to aid sleep and to calm down over-active children.

1 Lie down on the floor . . . lie on your back so that you are looking up at the ceiling. Now go stiff and hard all over . . . as hard as a board. That is very tense.

2 Now do the opposite, go loose and relaxed all over.

3 Shut your eyes . . . don't screw them up, just close them gently. Now have a secret talk to the different parts of your body to tell them to go tight first and then to relax. Don't say it out loud, just think it. Begin with your legs. Squeeze them together and press them down hard at the same time. They are hard and tense. Now tell them to relax, to go soft and loose. If you are doing it properly your legs flop outwards a bit and they feel heavy and loose.

4 Now tell your arms and hands to tighten up. Stretch out your fingers as wide as you can, then let them relax. Tell your fingers to go limp and still and loose. Then your arms become relaxed too and feel heavy and warm. Now tell your face to relax . . . to be a kind happy one . . . the sort of face that people like to look at. Make sure your lips aren't tight, just soft and hardly touching.

5 And now stay quiet and relaxed all over. When you get good at it, it's a lovely feeling and it makes the nasty feelings go away, and instead you feel calm and quiet.

6 If you feel comfortable, say slowly to yourself, 'I feel quiet . . . I feel relaxed.' Stay a little longer then have a good stretch and sit up SLOWLY and you'll feel fine.

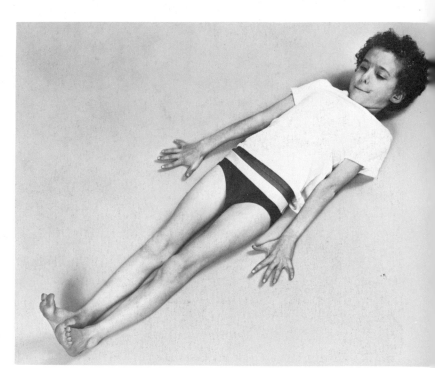

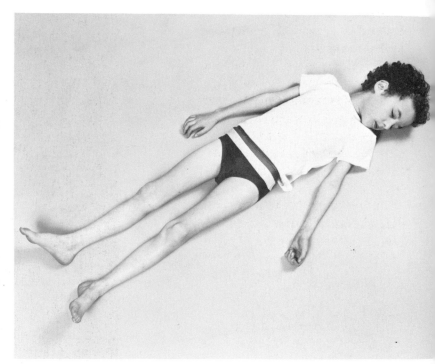

Working with groups

This makes a good quiet ending to a
lively physical education lesson. In
the beginning children will find lying
still difficult and strange, so only do it
for a very short time at first. Once they
get used to it and there is no fidgeting,
they settle down very quickly and you
can give them longer. Children can
test each other to check that limbs are
relaxed.

This will be the time to go on to
visualisation techniques if you think it
suitable.

MY SECRET PICTURE

Objective
To introduce simple visualisation techniques as a way of switching off unpleasant thoughts and putting happy ones in their place.

This is something a bit more difficult and not everyone can do it, but some people find it a great help especially if they are able to relax. It's called visualisation and is a way of sending nasty thoughts away and putting happy ones there instead.

1 Begin by relaxing all over in the way you have already learnt.

2 Now think of something that always makes you feel happy – it could be a special treasure of yours, or a pet, a place you love to be in, like the seaside or a garden, or a picture or a flower. These are only ideas. You choose your own secret happy picture. It will always be your special relaxing picture and no one else will have one quite like it. You needn't tell anyone what you have chosen because it is your own happy picture secret.

3 Now lie relaxed with your eyes closed and try to see it in your mind. Make the picture as clear as you can, but don't try too hard . . . just let it happen. How big is it? What are the colours like? What is specially good about it? Keep watching it as you relax. The picture may come and go but it gets easier as you practise. Keep the same picture every time. It makes you feel quietly happy as you watch it.

4 After a while, open your eyes, have a good stretch and sit up SLOWLY.

Suggestions for dance themes involving tensions and relaxation
(any age group)

Storm and gentle breeze (could be linked with growing plant theme)
Wooden doll and rag doll
Leaves blown by the wind to settle in a quiet place
Floating balloon which gradually leaks and collapses, or bursts suddenly
Curling smoke with sudden bursts of flame
Elastic stretched until it snaps
Shake the whole body, bouncing, twisting, wobbling, jerking, then try to repeat it in slow motion
Tin man and scarecrow (The Wizard of Oz)

Some teachers may prefer not to use imagery but to keep to 'pure' dance, introducing differing aspects of strength, lightness, sustained movement, sudden movement, stillness; in fact, all aspects of time, weight and space. Draw the children's attention to tension and relaxation so that they become familiar with the words associated with their feelings.

Suggestions for musical accompaniments to these dance are given in Appendix 1.

Profile: Middle years of childhood

This is the gang age, and a time when children are full of zest and energy, are avid for information and may read more than they ever will again. They rarely need rest but often require change. Most of the childhood infections are over and they play hard and sleep soundly. Many of them choose to be scruffy, reluctant to wash, cheeky, daring, and to them the opinion of the peer group and acceptance by them matters most. It is the age about which parents know least. They have single sex, short-lived secret societies composed of about six children, with their own dens, rituals, elaborate rules and daring exploits. Girls however may prefer two or three friends of their own sex rather than the group.

Belonging to the group becomes of great importance and to be rejected will cause stress and a loss of self-esteem. However, to be included means that others must be excluded: the 'in' group has to define who is 'out'. Children who are normally kind may become harshly hostile to those they reject. They hurl insults like 'Smelly', 'Fatty', 'Cissy' to establish their allegiance to the gang. The 'good' child may have the approval of adults but in being rejected by the peer group may be missing out on an important experience during this short phase of growing up. Their underlying loyalties and standards still belong to parents.

To capture the essence of this age group it is worth while trying to recall some of the rhymes and rituals you knew, which most children believe are secret and unique to them but which have been handed down by the spoken word over centuries, and some are common the world over. It has been possible to trace these games and chants back to the Middle Ages and beyond, and in the fifteenth-century painting *Children's Games* by the Flemish painter Breughel, you will find many of the games you played in this short span of middle childhood and which your children play today.

Girls have complicated skipping and ball game rhymes, ancient in origin but adapted with shrewd references to current affairs; boys have their rules of marbles and dabstones originating in Roman times, and both sexes enjoy the 'rude' rhymes and chants about teachers, policemen, lavatories and knickers, and they relish slapstick jokes and riddles. It is the age of 'It's not fair' because rules are considered to be inviolate; this represents a stage of moral development described by Jean Piaget the educational psychologist. These games and rituals illustrate the stage of growth and development of these children: the acquisition of intricate physical skills, a growing independence and development of ideas of what is just. There may be minor infringements with the law inspired by the gang (perhaps you too scrumped apples or knocked on doors and ran away), they may be insolent towards adults and this may be part of their growing towards independence, of discovering that they can stand up to authority. They are also learning what will not be tolerated.

Girls are noticeably two years ahead of boys in maturity and this may account for their different interests. They are more likely to form groups to collect for charity, act plays or produce exhibitions for adults to watch (for payment) and will show concern for younger children. But perhaps some of this is the result of society's expectations rather than the girls' choice.

These 9- to 13-year-olds are skill hungry now that they have developed control over the muscles of the body, and they are probably more nimble now than they ever will be again. They try out their skills with 'double-jointedness', going cross-eyed, doing handstands, cartwheels, waggling ears, juggling athletics and attempt adult games like football and tennis. They need every opportunity to let off steam in an acceptable manner with suitable physical activity. Challenges of the 'Can you do this?' kind are included in the techniques section.

Collecting becomes an important individual interest: badges, matchboxes, flowers, all varieties of objects are collected, classified and swapped. Parents may find the litter exasperating but these collections may well form the basis of a rewarding hobby or even a future career. It may become part of the incredible untidiness shown by many children especially boys of this age and the only comfort is that they do usually get better in a few years, and some psychologists have commented that the creative person may work best in conditions of cheerful disorder. Still, you do have your own rights and there are limits; don't think you are alone in having noisy untidy children, it is part of the characteristics of many in this age group.

Relaxation as a way of coping with anxiety is important now. Children of this age do have their fears and anxieties and this is often seen in their superstitious rituals to ward off evil. You may remember some of your own childhood tricks like crossing fingers when an ambulance passes, not treading on cracks in the pavement, rushing downstairs before the lavatory flushes, compulsive counting. They are now more anxious about achievement in class, being chosen for a team, doing well at sports and competitions and changing schools. The quick 'Calm down' relaxation exercise is useful now and the fact that it can be done without anyone noticing is particularly appreciated. The tension and relaxation exercises of the 'Can you do this?' kind are illustrated with single sex groups, with children working together in twos or threes. School becomes the ideal place to introduce these challenges in the physical education lesson, and classroom relaxation is useful to quieten down over-excited children.

The techniques – middle years of childhood

IRON MAN/WOMAN

Objectives

Strong tension in arms and legs followed by relaxation tested by partner. Later, to be able to isolate strong tension in groups of muscles without unnecessary tension in other parts of the body.

1 One partner lies on the ground facing upwards with one arm raised. The other partner tries to push the arm down against resistance (this involves very strong tension). Note how the whole body is involved: the other arm and hand and even the face becomes unnecessarily tense.

2 The arm is lowered and the partner lifts it to test for complete relaxation. It should feel loose, heavy and offer no resistance. Note how this affects the whole body.

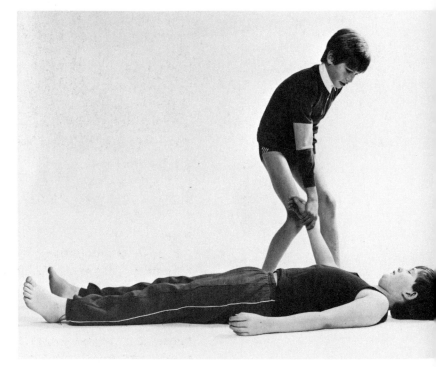

3 Repeat the exercise with a leg raised against resistance. This involves strong contraction of thigh and abdominal muscles.

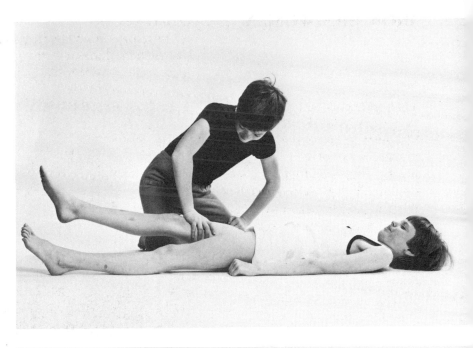

4 The leg is lowered and partner tests for relaxation by placing one hand under the knee and lifting the leg. It should feel heavy and unresisting.

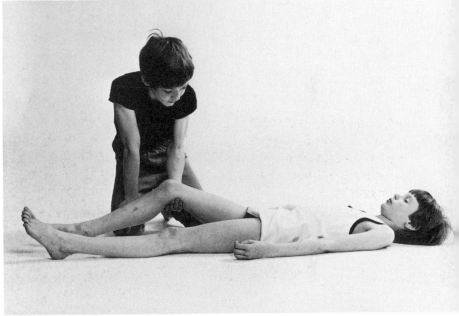

Notes
At first the whole body goes tense when one limb is strongly contracted. As children progress they should be able to contract one group of muscles without involving unnecessary tension elsewhere.

Grace and ease of movement is the result of an intricate interplay between muscle tension and relaxation. Children can discover when they are using unnecessary muscle tension which may spoil some of the physical skills they will learn later.

ROCKING THE DUMMY

Objective

A fun activity involving strong tension and cooperation between three children (boys or girls).

1 The 'dummy' stands with feet together between two supports, facing one of them. Supports stand with one foot forward, hands raised at shoulder level.

2 The dummy says 'Ready' and then falls forward towards the support facing him, keeping his whole body straight and strong. The support receives him with his palms on the dummy's shoulders and then pushes him towards the other support.

3 At first the supports should be quite close to the dummy to give confidence, but gradually move further away to make it more challenging. The dummy should remain straight with no bending of the body.

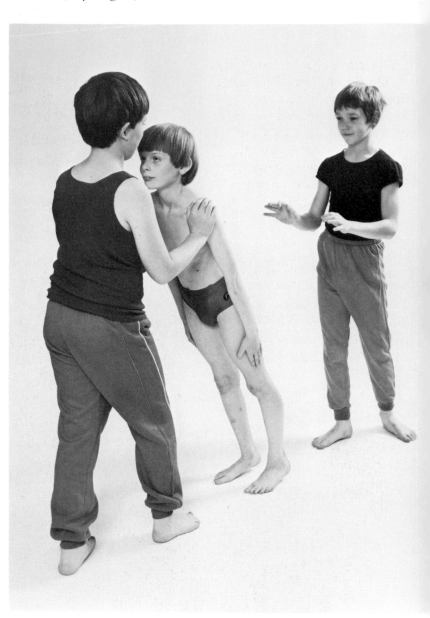

Notes

The dummy should always fall towards the facing support for the start of the rocking and be aware of whole body tension. In a class situation the supports' hands could touch the shoulders of the dummy to start the movement in order to give confidence.

This is fun as a beach or garden activity with the supports getting further and further away.

SHOULDER SHOVE

Objectives
A contest of strength involving pushing with tension in arms, shoulders and back.
Relaxation of arms is tested so that each child gains some appreciation of the characteristics of relaxed muscles.

1 Partners face each other with hands resting on each other's shoulders in front. They stand with one foot forward and begin by balancing lightly against each other. On the command 'GO' they each push steadily and strongly against each other until one has to give way.

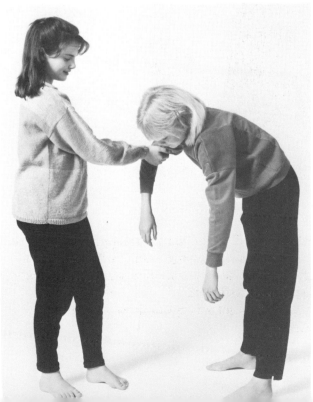

2 One partner leans forward with arms dangling loose and relaxed. The other partner tests for relaxation by placing one hand in front of the elbow and lifting the arm to feel its weight. The arm is allowed to drop, and if it is relaxed it falls immediately with no help or hindrance.

TURNING THE TURTLE

Objectives
For children to enjoy contests of strength in pushing, pulling and lifting.
To become aware of strong tension and then to be able to relax.
To assess the quality of relaxation by 'weighing' arms and legs.

1 One child becomes the turtle and lies face downwards on the ground, arms and legs spreadeagled sideways. All muscles are made strong and tense. His partner crouches or bends over him and attempts to roll him over, strongly resisted by the turtle.

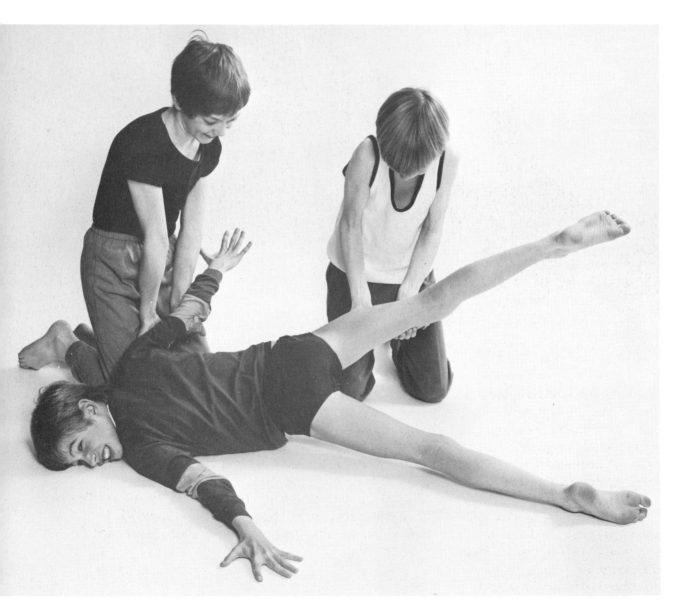

2 The turtle lies on his back, face upwards. His partner tests for relaxation in arms by first lifting one by the wrist and 'weighing' it, moving it about a little, then stands astride over the body of the turtle, takes both hands by the wrists and moves the arms with a swaying movement, assessing the weight and relaxation. Arms should feel heavy and loose and offer no resistance. The arms are then placed gently on the ground.

Notes
Children of this age enjoy the contests of strength involved in pulling, pushing and lifting. It is important that children should be evenly matched and they each have a turn.

These contests are very strenuous and short spells are better than long sustained efforts.

When working with a partner there should be an even, controlled start, so begin with each partner saying aloud 'One, two, three, GO'.

Draw attention to the welcome feeling of relaxation following the strenuous efforts.

THE TORMENTERS

Objectives
To demonstrate to children how it is possible to remain fully relaxed through a difficult experience.

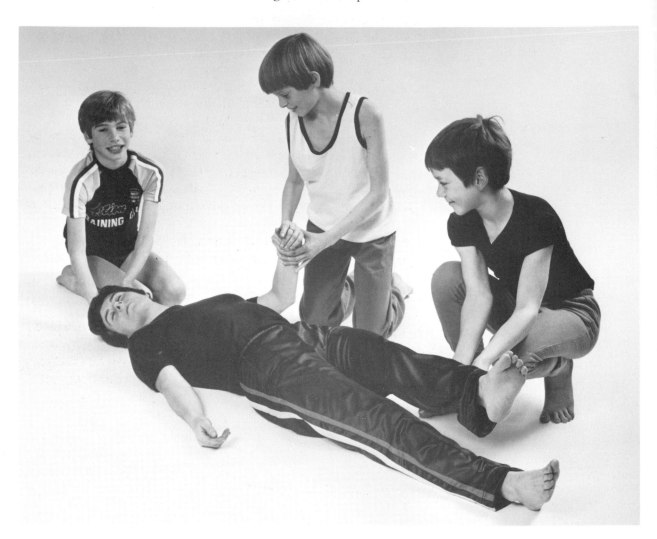

1 The parent or teacher lies on the ground in a fully relaxed position with arms a little away from the body, legs a little apart, eyes closed, mouth relaxed and a little open.
2 Three children become 'the tormenters' and test the relaxation by lifting and moving arms, legs, head. Other children observe. The movements must not be rough but the aim is to cause some tension in the adult.

Notes
At school, it will be necessary for the teacher to have a good relationship with the children, and considerable nerve and confidence to try this. It does have remarkably good results, especially if the teacher is able to relax well. It leads to profitable discussions on what relaxation involves and gives children a model of what they could achieve. It enhances the respect of the children for the adult and gives an excellent demonstration of the ability to relax through a difficult experience.

Later, when children are more skilled at relaxing, they can take turns at being tested by three others. This is also useful for older children and fun for parents to be involved in the testing.

CALM DOWN

Objectives

To give children a quick relaxation trick which can be used, unnoticed, whenever they are getting upset.

Instructions to individual child

This is a quick relaxation trick which you can use anywhere, at any time, without anyone noticing. You should learn some of the relaxation exercises first, especially for hands, shoulders and face.

1 As soon as you find yourself getting worked up or upset, say to yourself in a bossy sort of way 'Calm down'. That means telling your body to stop fussing and making you feel uncomfortable.

2 Then breathe in (not a lot) and then breathe out really SLOWLY, and as you do this, relax your hands. Don't think of anything else but this. Then breathe in again and as you breathe out this time, relax your jaw . . . make sure your teeth are not tightly together (because lots of people grit their teeth when they are angry or upset). Think just about this. Your hands and jaw are relaxed.

3 Then have two or three calm breaths and go on with what you are doing. There is no need to close your eyes for this trick so no one will notice.

When to use the calm down technique

Use it whenever you feel afraid or have to be brave, like when you have a cut knee dressed at school, or going to a new school, or changing classes, going to the dentist, going to hospital, before sports competitions, being in a play, being sent to the Head teacher. You will find many occasions when it will come in useful.

FULL RELAXATION

Instructions for parent or teacher

Starting position: this deeper relaxation can be practised sitting in a comfortable chair, lying in bed, lying on the floor or in the car on a long journey, perhaps with the help of a relaxation cassette.

At first it is best for children to learn lying down. Make sure the room is warm and there are no draughts. You will know best how to introduce this full relaxation technique so the following instructions are only a guide.

Instructions for children

1 Lie on your back with your legs a little apart and your arms a little away from your sides, fingers curved.

2 Begin by having a good stretch Stretch your fingers, your arms, your legs, your back – all tight and hard. Then breathe out and let the tension go. Have a few calm rhythmical breaths saying to yourself 'Relax' each time you breathe out. Close your eyes gently and continue with calm even breathing.

3 Tell each part of your body to go loose and floppy and limp. Begin with your feet, because a lot of people wriggle their toes and ankles when they are anxious. Then tell your legs to relax – you'll find that they roll outwards when they are relaxed. Now your fingers – tell them to go floppy and limp and still. You'll soon find that your arms begin to feel heavy and warm.

Now your face – let it be a soft face, not frowning, not with your mouth tight or teeth together, but a relaxed nearly smiling face with your lips soft. Now just stay like this, still, comfy and loose. And soon this makes you feel comfortable inside too, it makes you feel quiet and calm, and it's a lovely dreamy comfy feeling.

Once you feel relaxed, say to yourself slowly 'I feel calm . . . I feel relaxed', and then try to relax even further than before.

4 Now, if you like it, go on to the visualisation techniques described earlier (see p. 41). Choose your own pleasant picture to look at in your mind and stay watching it while you relax. Stay for at least six minutes. If you are doing this before you go to sleep at night you will find that you sleep more peacefully, but if you have to stop now, open your eyes, have a good stretch, perhaps a yawn and a wriggle, then sit up SLOWLY.

Notes for parents and teachers

Your voice is important; try to feel relaxed yourself and speak slowly and clearly (because the children have their eyes closed and cannot see you). There is no need for a droning hypnotic voice, nor a whispering one; just use your ordinary speaking voice but make it as calm as you can and have good pauses between instructions. Don't walk around while you are talking.

Draw the children's attention to the idea that they now have a method under their own control, no one else's, to help them manage disturbing feelings.

Notice any child who appears unable to let go or who is very fidgety because this sometimes indicates that the child has special anxieties. Five to six minutes is sufficient for them to get the sensation of relaxing. A brief spell of about two minutes at the end of a physical education lesson will make it more likely that they will go quietly to the next class.

ALTERNATIVE POSITIONS FOR GENERAL RELAXATION

Objective
To try different positions for general relaxation so that the most appropriate can be selected to suit the individual and occasion.

1 Lying on your back: arms are a little away from the body, fingers curved, legs a little apart, ankles rolled outwards, head resting easily in the middle. Heavier older children may wish to have a cushion under the head. Children who feel too strange with arms not touching the body may prefer to rest hands on the abdomen. This gives a feeling of security until they feel more confident.

2 'Coachman' position: sit on a chair or stool with feet resting on the ground just underneath the knees. Lean forward so that elbows rest firmly on knees taking the weight off the back as it leans forward. Hands hang limp and loose, the head drops forward.

3 Leaning on the desk: feet rest on the floor under the knees, thighs roll outwards a little, fingers relaxed (i.e. not making a fist), head rests on forearms or hands.

4 In the back of the car: sit well back with head resting back on support, fingers resting on lap, with one hand cradled in the other.

Notes

The deepest relaxation will be produced using the lying down position with the whole body supported. When practising, this is better on the floor because the comfort of a bed induces sleep before full attention has been paid to relaxing each part of the body.

The 'coachman' position is suitable in between periods of study, or between breaks in physical activity, for example between sets at tennis.

Leaning on the desk can be used in class for a brief quietening down session or before undertaking creative activity.

Children who become restless on a long car journey will be helped by some of the stretching and contracting activities (shoulders, legs, face, hands) before full relaxation. Use a cassette if it helps. You could make one of your own or use a commercially made one for children.

Teenagers and students

Between the ages of 14 and 18 there are astonishing but normal differences in growth, development and maturity as teenagers move from childhood to becoming adults, so a universal profile is impossible. In the same class at school there may be some who are still little children while others look like teachers, and both early and late maturers will have their own special problems to face.

Girls will have completed their growth in height by about 17, but boys will go on until 20, and even after that slight growth may continue for several years. The major spurt in growth lasts about two and a half years and during this time all parts of the body are involved: bones, organs, muscles, glands, skin, even eyes and it may cause consternation that growth is so uneven and some parts grow faster than others. The feet and hands grow first before the arms and legs and girls may wonder if their enormous feet will ever stop growing. The nose reaches its mature stage before the mouth and jaw and the hair line recedes. This temporary imbalance may cause much anxiety and mirror gazing. The skin which was thin and transparent in childhood now becomes thicker, and the sweat glands associated with sexual maturity produce an increase of perspiration with a more intense odour. The sweat glands overact at times of stress causing embarrassment to the teenager and may also contribute to acne. As the stomach grows larger and there are metabolic changes in the body, teenagers often have enormous appetites.

Early maturers

Early maturing boys have a great advantage. Since prestige is closely linked with athleticism at this age the bigger stronger boy will gain in self-confidence, is more independent and is often chosen as a leader. On the other hand, the early maturing girl, wearing her new body shape with unease, may find she is expected to be more responsible than she is yet ready to be, or she may be considered 'fast'. She may become shy about showering after physical education lessons and begin to dislike games and athletics.

Late maturers

A late-maturing boy is likely to be under some stress. He may be dominated by his fellows, be chosen last for the team, have feelings of inadequacy and may not be granted the independence given to the others. It would be a help for him to know that according to James Tanner, author of *Growth at Adolescence*, late developers will usually reach a greater height than the early maturers in the end, and they often turn out to be more friendly and more understanding as a result of having coped with their own difficulties. Teachers and parents should be on the look out for the late-maturing boy and help him build up his self-esteem in other directions. He needs to find something at which he can excel, will absorb his interest and give him the approval of his peers.

Changes in emotion and behaviour

The dramatic glandular and physical changes inevitably affect behaviour in different ways. The teenager who lolls about, appears to be indolent, won't help at home, is not different from many others of this age and may be reacting to temporary emotional and physical fatigue. It is not just sheer cussedness. They may appear to be impervious to the feelings of others closely associated with them, yet they may be passionately concerned about great causes. Their self-absorption is part of the search for identity which in some way we had to experience. This stage will pass and most teenagers who are irritating and do daft things grow up to be responsible caring adults.

The swings of moods from elation to depression are part of the glandular changes and there are some positive benefits. Never again will there be such a surge of ecstasy, an awareness of beauty, and heightened creativity, but there can also be severely black moods and depression, and today's problems of unemployment add to anger and frustration and increase the depression.

Some conflict with parents is probably inevitable because there are two main problems for the teenager: coming to terms with new sexual feelings and the drive for independence. But conflict need not be alienation and the door can always be left open for reconciliation. Save the clashes for something really worth while and not for minor issues. Don't be hurt by their criticisms and use your relaxation techniques to avoid the conflicts making you upset, give teenagers as much responsibility as you can, then enjoy their increasing independence and your growing freedom.

Relaxation

All teenagers need privacy, but although solitude can be a relaxing refuge, one of the greatest causes of stress for young men and women is loneliness, and the worst form is to be lonely in a crowd. Never push a shy youngster into social situations he or she cannot manage. Support them by introducing some techniques for gaining confidence.

They will be helped by learning to relax, using visualisation to rehearse their behaviour in a social situation or at interviews, then adults can help them to go one step at a time to gain confidence until they feel free and at ease. It really works, but it is best to begin early.

Relaxation will also be useful for 'psyching up' before competitive events, taking exams, going to the dentist, taking the first driving test, making a date, coping with sleeplessness and recovering from fatigue.

In the early teenage years relaxation is best learnt in school as part of physical education, but later it will be more effective if it is learnt with a friend who will assess tension and relaxation, and then it should be practised regularly alone.

Older children may be ready to go on to other quieting techniques, but these should be very simple because if they become very involved in meditation without supervision they may experience disturbing sensations. For most children progressive relaxation learnt as a physical skill and applied to daily living situations is all they need for stress and tension control.

The techniques –
teenagers and students

Introduction for teenagers

You can adapt many of the techniques suggested for the younger age groups, especially those for hands and shoulders, but by now there will usually be no need to tighten up muscles hard before relaxing. You just start from where you are and relax further. Try to recognise a degree of tension by tightening muscles only just the amount you do when you are anxious or excited: it's like turning on the radio just enough to hear it, but no more than that. Then let the tension go, recognise the change in your joints and muscles then relax even a little more. If you are not sure whether you really are relaxing you can try out some of the suggestions for measuring the effects of relaxing shown later.

Once you have learnt, try to apply the techniques to daily living situations, and perhaps you can help your friends too.

Although you can relax through noise and discomfort, it is very difficult if you are cold, so when you practise see that the room is warm.

There are two ways you can use relaxation:

1 *Tension control* – this means using only the amount of effort needed for doing a job well, and keeping your energy for the things that really matter.

2 *Stress control* – using it to cope with difficult situations, anxiety and worry and to help you sleep.

This involves:

1 Recognising unnecessary tension and releasing it in everyday situations.

2 A quick relaxation technique you can use anywhere in an emergency.

3 Short 'time out' spells of relaxation, lasting not more than five minutes (can even be less).

4 Deep relaxation, when the mind idles gently and removes itself from its problems. This practice should last about twenty minutes. You can learn relaxation like any other physical skill, so try to practise every day until it becomes part of you.

CALM BREATHING

Objectives

To check on correct breathing and avoid problems of hyperventilation.
To use as a quick relaxation method.
To use as a prelude to relaxation practice.

Introduction

The way you feel is closely linked with how you breathe. When you are anxious, your breathing is faster and irregular and takes place in the upper part of the chest. When you are relaxed the breathing is done primarily by the diaphragm so that the abdomen rises as you breathe in. This makes more room for the intake of air and as a result the breathing is slow and rhythmical. When you are at rest, calm breathing has a rate of about 6 to 10 breaths a minute, but when you are upset it could be 16 per minute or more, even when you are resting. By breathing calmly, slowly and rhythmically you will feel more relaxed.

Taking very deep breaths or breathing fast when you are at rest is a great mistake, and can cause hyperventilation. This simply means overbreathing and this can upset the balance of the chemicals in the blood by getting rid of too much carbon dioxide. This can make you feel strange and even more anxious. So it makes sense to check up to see whether you are breathing correctly when you are resting. (Your body looks after your breathing when you are active so there is no need to bother about that.) If you find that you are overbreathing, pay attention to a SLOW breath out rather than a big breath in. Otherwise, once you have checked, forget about your breathing and just let it happen naturally.

1 Sit or lie comfortably and place one hand on top of your abdomen and the other on your upper chest in front.
2 Take in a breath (not too much) and your lower hand should rise first and the top one hardly at all. It looks as if your abdomen is filling up with air.
3 Breathe out slowly as you relax and your abdomen lowers.

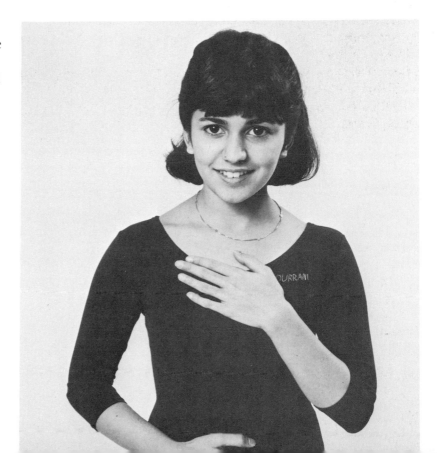

HANDS

Objectives
To recognise individual patterns of tension in hands and become aware of the link between this tension and general stress. To use appropriate tension and relaxation of hands in everyday situations.

Tension

1 Clench your fists so that your knuckles show white.
2 Stretch out your fingers as far as you can.
3 Tighten your hands in the special way you do when you are anxious (if you don't know this, ask your friends or family: they will almost certainly have noticed).

Relaxation

1 Shake your hands loose.
2 Rest your hands lightly on your lap so that one hand is cradled in the other with your fingers and thumb relaxed and gently curved (you are less likely to grip them tightly in this position). Or if you prefer rest them on the arms of the chair. Notice how relaxation of hands helps you to feel calm.

Notice how other people show their tension in hands. Some wring their hands, or grip their thumbs, pick at their nails, do 'pill rolling', drum fingers on the table or arm of the chair or stretch fingers out wide and tense.

Then become aware of tension in your own hands during the day and relax them when you can, e.g. when you are watching TV, sometimes in class, at social occasions when you are not quite sure of yourself, and whenever you are anxious. You will find this awareness of unnecessary tension useful if you play a musical instrument or have intricate jobs to do. It helps too when you have to speak in public. When you are relaxed your fingers often become warmer and some people can even show this rise in temperature by using a sensitive thermometer strapped to fingers

CHAIROPLANE ARM SHAKE

Objectives
To relax arms and to give feelings of general relaxation. To loosen tension in arms before swimming races.

To use as quick winding down activity

Chairoplane

1 Stand with your feet astride and your arms hanging loosely by your sides. Twist your trunk so that you face first one way then the other so that your arms float round you. They remain heavy and loose. Vary the speed so that they float lazily round, then as you move faster they flap against your sides. Notice the feeling of relaxation in your arms.

Arm shake

1 Lean a little way forward with your arms dangling down. Shake your arms from the wrist upward to shoulders, all the muscles loose and relaxed and they wobble. Repeat standing upright.

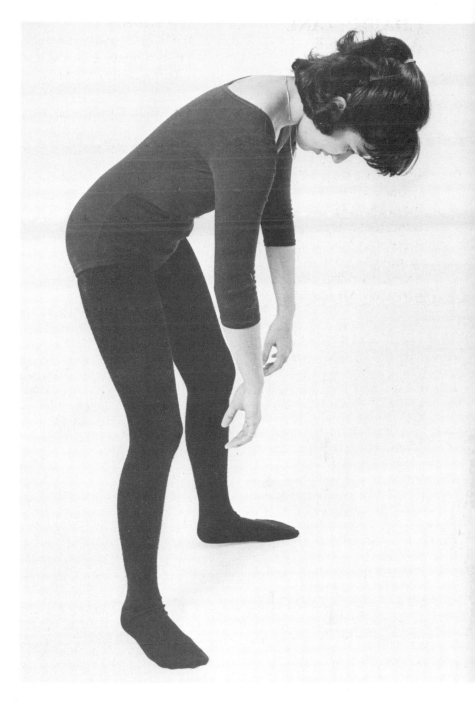

Notes
The 'chairoplane' exercise has been found to help in releasing general tension and can be used either as a quick winding down exercise or as a prelude to general relaxation.

The arm shake is used by swimmers to release unnecessary tension before a race. It also helps release tension before work requiring dexterity or to relieve tension after hard manual work.

SHOULDER RELAXATION

Objective
To recognise tightness in shoulders in everyday living situations and release the tension.

Note
If you always hold your shoulders tight and hunched it gives people the impression that you are tense and nervous, so try to correct this before it becomes a habit that is difficult to break.

Try to notice unnecessary tension in your shoulders in everyday situations, like watching television, writing, sitting in a class or in a bus, learning to drive. Then let the tension go.

If you have a concentrated period of working release the tension by moving your shoulders about, but do this before they begin to ache.

1 Sit or stand upright and tighten up your shoulders slightly, but only the amount you do when you are anxious or over alert. Recognise this as something you often do in difficult situations, and then release it by letting your shoulders drop.

2 Let your shoulders drop even further by pulling them down and at the same time make your neck long. Then let your shoulders relax comfortably.

3 Release tension by movement. Shrug your shoulders up and down, then wriggle them about until they feel relaxed and easy. Stay for a while and become aware of the position of your shoulders and neck when they are relaxed.

4 Check in the mirror or get a partner to see whether one shoulder is higher than the other (this sometimes happens if you are a tennis player) and you must take care not to let it become a permanent habit.

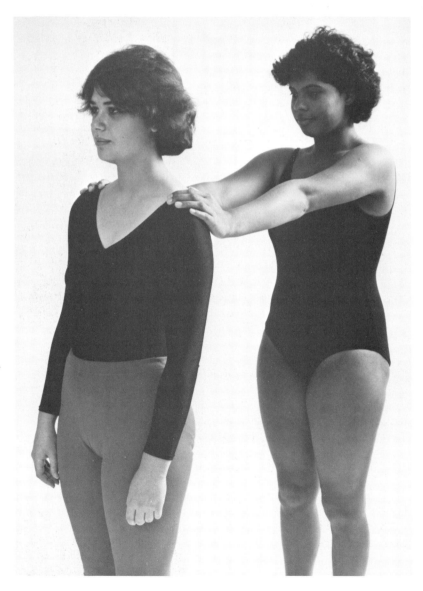

FACE POSTURE

Objective
To detect unnecessary facial tension and to correct faulty posture using a mirror.

1 Stand in front of a mirror and frown. Raise your eyebrows and frown at the same time (difficult but it gives a picture of anguish, and anxiety). Notice how this makes you look to other people and how just doing this can make you feel tense.

Now, let the tension go (some face massage helps, see p. 121) so that your forehead feels smooth. Notice how this makes you feel calmer.

2 Tighten your lips, then let them relax. Imagine you are about to smile so that your face looks pleasant and relaxed. Make sure your teeth are not tightly together (making circular movements with your fingertips round your mouth will help relax the muscles; this is something many models do before being photographed).

3 Thrust your head forward in an aggressive pose. Notice how this looks and see how it also affects your posture. Feel behind your neck with one hand and notice how hard and tense the muscles are. Then let your head rest in an easy balanced position so that your neck is long without being tense.

4 Check in the mirror whether your posture is good. Stand tall and easy; shoulders should be level, your head held in the middle and not on one side (notice how many people do hold the head this way causing strain on the neck muscles). Notice how this looks. Good upright posture not only makes you look confident, but it makes you feel it, too, and your clothes will fit better.

'STOP'
A QUICK RELAXATION TECHNIQUE

This is a quick relaxation technique which is useful in an emergency, and no one will notice what you are doing. When you realise that you are getting worked up, say sharply to yourself 'STOP' (i.e. 'stop fussing').

Take a breath in, then breathe out SLOWLY, and as you do so relax your shoulders and hands. Pause for a moment.

Take another breath and this time as you breathe out relax your lips and jaw (because many people grit their teeth when they are frustrated and upset). Breathe in again and as you breathe out slowly, say to yourself, 'I FEEL CALM . . . I FEEL RELAXED.'

This works surprisingly well if you have practised beforehand and you can use it at social occasions, before interviews, before competing if you are too worked up, before public speaking. There will be many occasions when it will help.

DEEP RELAXATION

Objectives

To combat mental and physical tension by muscle relaxation.

To enable the mind to switch off from problems without reducing alertness or drive.

To use the technique in preparation for athletic and competitive events, and as a prelude to other quieting methods. To overcome staleness after intensive training.

1 Try to find somewhere free from distractions. The deepest relaxation comes when you are lying down, but you can manage quite successfully sitting in a comfortable chair. If you are lying down, lie on your back with arms and legs a little away from your sides. (You may prefer to lie with your hands resting on top of your abdomen if relaxation seems strange at first.)

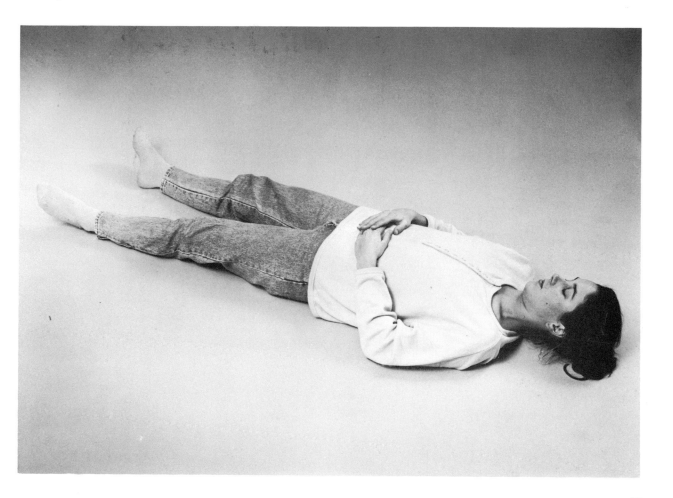

If you are sitting in a chair, sit so that your back is well supported, and rest your head back if the chair is high enough. Place both feet on the floor and rest your arms along the arm of the chair or on your lap.

2 Have a good stretch, arms, fingers, back, neck, legs, then settle down. Snuggle down until you are comfortable. Breathe in (not a very deep breath) and then breathe out slowly. Do this again and as you do so, close your eyes gently and feel the tension beginning to drain away. Then go back to your ordinary breathing, calm and even.

3 Focus your thoughts on each part of your body in turn, to the muscles and joints.

Relax your toes and ankles.

Relax your legs so that your thighs roll outwards.

Feel your back touching the floor or the back of the chair. Let this do all the supporting so that your back muscles relax.

Relax your hands so that your fingers are curved, limp and floppy. Quite still.

Relax your shoulders, let them drop.

Let your head rest easily against the support so that the neck muscles relax.

Relax your face, let the expression come off it so that your lips are soft, your teeth are not tightly together, your forehead is smooth.

Stay like this for a little while and capture the whole body sensation of relaxing. You may begin to feel warm and your limbs heavy. Then there may be a sensation of floating. Don't be surprised by these feelings, just enjoy them as part of relaxing.

When you begin to feel

comfortable and peaceful say to yourself, 'I feel relaxed . . . I feel calm.' Register this feeling. Remind yourself that relaxation relieves fatigue because it is only when muscles are relaxed that they are really resting, and it relieves mental tension because you cannot be very anxious and relaxed at the same time.

Have at least six more minutes relaxing like this.

If it suits you you can go on to some of the quieting techniques described later.

If you are practising before you sleep you will discover that you drop off more easily and your sleep is more peaceful. But if you have to finish after your six minutes, open your eyes and look around, have a good stretch and then sit up SLOWLY.

Notes

You cannot of course relax and read this at the same time, so get the gist of it and then try on your own, or better still make a cassette for yourself, or use a commercially produced one, or get a friend to read the instructions for you until you are ready to practise on your own. Try to have a spell of deep relaxation every day. If you are serious about it you will practise for at least ten minutes twice a day. Don't make an effort to relax, or try hard . . . just let it happen. Some people feel that music helps. If you want to use it, wait until you have got used to the idea of deep relaxation then choose music with a slow beat . . . something like Handel's 'Largo' is ideal because it has a beat of 60 a minute, which is the rate of a calm heartbeat and helps you feel quiet. Once you have chosen, keep to the same piece of music so that it becomes associated with calmness and relaxation. At the beginning you may find you are restless after only a few minutes. Stop trying, but next time have a little longer. It takes at least six minutes to get the feelings of deep relaxation and this comes gradually. When you have got it it becomes a skill you will be glad to use all your life.

QUIETING
(or thought diversion)

Objectives

To select from various techniques a way of diverting the mind from troubled thoughts.

To have periods of refreshing mental rest free from care.

Instructions

1 *Counting colours* – when travelling to school, interviews or anywhere that causes anxiety, count everything you can see of a certain colour, e.g. look for everything coloured yellow: vans, posters, doors, clothes, flowers. Concentrate on this. It is surprising how observant you can become noting coloured objects you had previously ignored.

2 *Visualising* – while you are relaxing, visualise something or somewhere that gives you pleasure. Focus your thoughts on this and make the picture as clear in your mind as you can. Always choose the same picture. If other thoughts intrude, just acknowledge them, let them pass, and go back to your own visualisation. Don't try hard, just let it happen.

3 *Listening to a sound* – (a 'mantra') when you are relaxed, focus your mind on a sound, invent a word that has no meaning like 'Toomba' or 'Whishna' and quietly think your word slowly over and over again. If your mind wanders, gently bring it back to the sound.

4 *Focus on your breathing* – count the first breath as 'one', then continue counting each outbreath until you reach ten, then start again.

Or breathe in and out slowly saying 'in', 'out' (slowly), 'relax' (as you pause).

5 *Kinaesthetic awareness* – become aware of each part of your body as it relaxes. Notice how it feels, notice the pressures of the floor or chair. If your mind wanders, switch it back to feelings of bodily relaxation.

Notes

'Quieting' is the modern term for a method of relaxing known for centuries. It is often referred to as meditation. Different people respond to different methods: some have good visual imagery, some may have a keen kinaesthetic memory and respond to physical feelings, while others do best by focusing on a sound or prefer the objective method of counting breathing. It makes sense to try several methods, but once one has been chosen, it should not be changed. If this method of quieting suits you it will require regular practice, say fifteen minutes a day, and should be combined with muscle relaxation.

PSYCHING UP and WARMING DOWN

Objective

To aid mental and emotional preparation for competitive events and for 'warming down' afterwards.

Instructions

Psyching up

1 Make a habit of recalling any uplifting and successful experiences you have had in training or competition. Do this as soon as possible after the event using all your senses: recall the sounds (perhaps the spectators, your feet pounding, your breathing, the ball on your racquet), the physical feelings (your muscles, the wind, contact with players), smell (grass, a nearby factory, chalk). Make the recall as vivid as possible so that you can repeat it mentally later.

2 Use relaxation and visualisation as part of your preparation away from the event. Relax fully, then have a mental rehearsal of the activity. See yourself performing skilfully and confidently. Watch yourself taking part and use all your senses. Visualise the performance at the speed you would use (e.g. if it is to be a sprint you could even time it so that you see yourself at peak performance). Sometimes rehearse mentally only the important part of the activity you wish to improve.

At first, alternate the visualisation and relaxation, a few minutes of each, not more. As you get better you can do this quickly.

Practise this for not more than five minutes a day for five days a week.

3 Just before the event, find a quiet place and warm up mentally using the quick relaxation technique and visualise yourself in an important part of the activity. You can do this also in breaks during the event (some top class tennis players do this between sets).

Warming down

After the event you will probably be 'high' with excitement. It is just as important to warm down mentally as it is physically so that you avoid the ill-effects of keeping the arousal high. Use relaxation, calm breathing, warm baths, massage to help you quieten down. This will help you not to get stale as a result of intensive training.

Notes

These methods are also useful for musicians, actors, public speakers and as part of assertion training.

Some objective measures of relaxation

These objective measurements are interesting to older pupils and help to make sense of learning to relax.

1 **Weighing arms, legs, head** – when a partner lifts them they should feel heavy if the muscles are relaxed, and there should be no resistance to the movement.

2 **Feeling muscle tension by touch** – with one hand reach across to the upper part of the opposite arm. Tighten that arm a little and feel how the muscles become hard and tense. Then let the arm drop and relax and feel the difference. The muscles feel soft and you can get hold of handfuls when they are relaxed.

3 **Change in pulse rate** – take your own pulse first. Tuck the elbow of your right arm into your waist, resting your forearm straight in front of you, fingers uppermost. Place the first two fingers of your left hand on the right side of your wrist, about 1 inch below the mound at the base of your thumb. Count the number of beats for half a minute, then multiply by two. Do this before and after relaxing. When you can do this easily test your partner before and after at least six minutes of relaxing. The pulse rate is usually markedly slower.

4 **Change in respiration rate** – the relaxing partner lies face upwards with a piece of folded card resting on the chest (this is so that partners can observe the breathing rate from a distance). Partners record the breathing rate before and after at least six minutes of relaxing. (It is usually slower.)

5 **Change in finger temperature** – a sensitive thermometer is strapped to a finger before relaxing and a reading taken. After relaxing for at least fifteen minutes another reading is taken. A slight rise in finger temperature often occurs after deep relaxation.

6 **Change in blink rate** – this is not very reliable, but with some people the blink rate is fast when they are tense and slow when they are relaxed. Observe a partner unobtrusively during the day and count the blink rate. Then do the same after a period of relaxation.

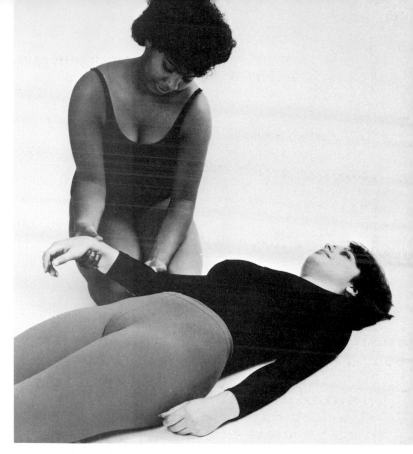

7 **Using biofeedback apparatus** – the most useful form of biofeedback is a skin resistance galvanometer with audible feedback. This is a fascinating method of demonstrating the bodily effects of stress and it shows how the user can exert some voluntary control over internal states. I recommend it as a tool for the teacher to demonstrate the effects of stress and relaxation, but it will not be necessary for individual pupils to acquire the apparatus to learn to relax.

Electrodes are attached to two fingers of the user and the apparatus switched on. The sound it makes gives feedback of information about general arousal. In states of anxiety or excitement there is a change in the electrical resistance of the skin: this is caused by the response of the sweat glands to stress (though the sweating is so slight that you may be unaware of it) and this makes the pitch of the sound rise. When you are relaxed the sound lowers to a growl and you may be able to make it die away altogether. By using this type of apparatus it is possible to monitor the stress response and find ways of gaining control over it.

A sharp clap and a shout by the teacher or partner will send the sound rising. This is the normal reaction to a threat. Asking the user to recall an alarming or humiliating event will also make the pitch rise, even though the 'threat' is only imaginary. But asking the user to spell 'rhythm' backwards in front of the class may make the sound rise even higher: in this case the threat was to self-esteem. This illustrates that the same survival reaction to a threat to life is produced unnecessarily for things that are imaginary or for fears of what other people may think of us.

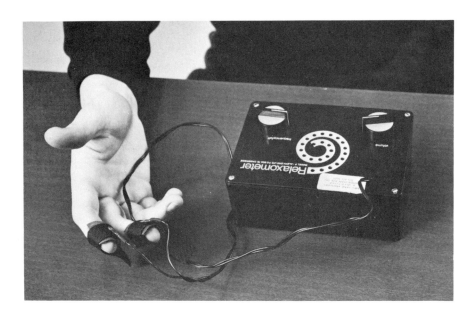

Note
In addition to these objective methods pupils should be encouraged to discuss their subjective feelings after applying relaxation techniques to daily living situations.

Relaxation in the school curriculum

Many subjects in school can either directly or indirectly be involved in teaching about the management of stress: e.g. physical education, human biology and physiology, home economics, health education, physics (making biofeedback apparatus, thermometers). It is also useful for school counsellors to help over-stressed pupils (and staff) and to careers guidance teachers, to give help with coping with interviews.

6

Suggested study routines for students

Most teenagers have to face the pressures of examinations, and many parents will share these strains too, because on the results may depend future careers. These pressures may be intense and sometimes un-reasonable, and if they are not well managed they can cause disruption of social and emotional life, not only for themselves but the whole family.

The arts of studying and revising can be learnt as a set of skills, and the training should start long before major examinations are imminent. In learning these skills, relaxation and the support of friends and adults play a useful role.

How to study effectively

Plan your programme

Try to balance work and recreation, and plan so that you have at least one whole day off from study as well as another evening or half day for recreation. Don't drop all your physical activities: they are now important for your health and study. Make a large timetable and put in your deadlines for essays, projects and revision, social activities and include some time for relaxation practice. Put the chart up where your parents and friends can see it.

Try to have a special work place

Whether it has to be the kitchen table, a corner of the library, your bedroom or a study make it a place associated with work and make it as welcoming as possible. It should be well lit, adequately warm and, as far as possible, free from distractions. Your parents may deplore any background music, but if it is continuous and kept at a low level it does appear to help some students, it cuts out other distracting sounds and may even aid concentration so long as it does not demand attention. However some students will find that music interferes with serious study.

Don't procrastinate

You are likely to become a victim of your own procrastination rituals, like telephoning friends, eating snacks, trying a new hairstyle, playing music, in fact anything to put off working. Recognise why you are doing this and try to get down to work immediately you close the door of your room. Do something *at once* and don't find excuses or reasons for not working.

Practise rapid reading and skimming

Reading skills have more relevance to academic attainment than anything else. Speed is important and is a skill that can be learnt. The average adult reads silently at 240 words a minute, but with training this can be raised to 360 or more words a minute without losing comprehension. Anxious people often read slowly, afraid to miss a word, or sometimes this may be a hang over from early school reading when every word was vocalised. One method of teaching rapid reading includes relaxation. A short spell of full relaxation is followed by reading a paragraph as quickly as possible, letting the eye take in half a line at a time rather than individual words. This is followed by a test of comprehension. Repeated practice will speed up reading and becomes a skill of lifetime value.

Skimming a book is necessary for effective study so that relevant material can be selected without wasting time. Scan the table of contents, flip over the book to read chapter headings, glance at illustrations and charts, read short extracts to get the hang of the book as a whole. Then you will be able to select what material is relevant.

Teach someone else

The best way of learning is to teach the things you can't remember or understand to someone else. Play the role of teacher and prepare a mini lesson with all the visual aids, notes, diagrams you can muster and teach your friend. You will find it is impossible to forget the contents of this particular lesson. Then try to become a 'getter' as well as a 'giver' by letting your friend teach you something different and you both should ask questions about the bits you don't understand. This can be a rewarding experience for you both. If you are both getting worked up and fatigued, have a brief spell of activity and then relax for five minutes, using a cassette if it helps. You will find you are refreshed and can think more clearly.

Motivation

Lack of motivation causes apathy and lack of purpose. If you are to believe it is worthwhile giving up some leisure activities and interests in order to study you really need to find a good reason. Dr Wankowski, when he studied why some students fail, found that those who had a clearer picture of their intended future than others were more likely to succeed. Sometimes, just by working hard on a disliked subject an interest grows, or sometimes a knowledgeable friend or adult can share with you some of the enthusiasm you are missing. Make your learning as active as possible: if the textbook is your own make pencil notes in it, underline, make pencil notes in the margin, query something you don't understand. It often helps you to remember things if you make drawings, illustrate with charts, ask and answer questions, or even make up silly rhymes or songs about the subject. Keep notes on small cards which you can keep in your pocket or bag and refer to them whenever you have an odd moment during the day. The more active your learning the more interesting it becomes and remembering becomes easier.

Relaxation releases excessive tension and helps study

Over-anxiety acts as a block to comprehension and remembering, and excessive muscle tension interferes with writing and manual dexterity as well as causing aches and pains in muscles. When you think that you have no time to relax it is probably when you need it most. It doesn't take long once you have learnt and will help in your learning process.

When you have been writing or typing for a while, break off, shake your fingers loose, give your hands a quick massage, so that they feel relaxed again. After about forty-five minutes of study, break off for about five minutes and release the tension with activity: have a good stretch, wriggle your shoulders and have a quick two minute relaxation practice. Don't break off for a long time if you are in the middle of a special topic, but in between different subjects take longer. Breaks allow the mind to integrate material.

If the study has been particularly demanding and stressful, and you are getting worked up about it, take some vigorous exercise to use up the stress chemicals: run up and downstairs a few times, go for a jog, do some exercises to music, or dance to relieve the tension. Then sit in a chair or lie on the floor and have five or more minutes of full 'time out' relaxation. This will clear your mind and give you a fresh start.

When you have to write a long essay or project and have done all the preliminary gathering of material and it seems a muddle, leave the papers spread around and have a good twenty minutes of time out for relaxation. This is not sleep but conscious muscle relaxation and mind quieting. After this passive awareness it is surprising how everything seems to fall into place and you can go ahead and write it up. Relaxation breaks really do improve learning and relieve anxiety and could well become part of school preparation for examinations.

After studying in the evening, have at least half an hour to wind down before you go to bed. If you have difficulty in getting off to sleep, stop work an hour before bedtime and switch off your active mind with pleasant reading, watching TV, or keeping up one of your hobbies. Then when you are in bed, practise full body muscle relaxation and calm breathing before you sleep.

STUDY BREAK

If your study has been very frustrating or has been intensive for some time, or if you feel fidgety, anxious and tense, break off from work for a while and have a good stretch, to release muscle tension and help ward off fatigue. If you feel particularly worked up, do some vigorous exercise:

1 Run up and downstairs three or four times so that you become a bit breathless. Or
2 Go for a short jog.
3 Put on some music and dance to it.
4 Do some vigorous exercises.
5 Then follow this with a quick relaxation practice.

Objective
To release tension during intensive study sessions by vigorous activity and relaxation.

Notes
This should only be a short break so that you don't lose your motivation for work, but it does help to dispel feelings of anxiety and tension and you are likely to do better work when you settle again.

TIME OUT

To provide a quick relaxation break in between studying, before a party, when over-anxious about competing, after coming in tired.

1 Sit in a chair with your back well supported. Breathe in and have a good stretch. Breathe out and snuggle back comfortably. Have two calm breaths (think: 'In, out, relax').
2 Close your eyes or just look downwards and focus your thoughts on each part of your body in turn. Always keep to the same order: right ankle and leg, left ankle and leg (thighs roll outwards); left hand, right hand (fingers limp, curved and still); left arm, right arm (they feel heavy); abdomen (moves easily as you breathe); face (cheeks soft, lips hardly touching, forehead relaxed).
3 Stay relaxed for the rest of the five minutes and become aware of the whole body sensation in muscles and joints. Say slowly to yourself, 'I feel relaxed . . . I feel calm.'
4 When the five minutes are up, have a good stretch, look around and get back to work refreshed.

Notes
Some people find it a help to tighten muscles strongly before relaxing each part, but try to dispense with this as soon as you can because it sometimes makes you feel more anxious. Once you have learnt to relax the best way of practising is to begin from where you are and then relax further. It is like turning on the radio so that you can only just hear it, then turning it off gradually so that it becomes silent.

When you get to college

One of the hardest things to do when you arrive at college is to learn how to study, how to structure your learning and how to discipline yourself. Unlike in school, where the staff usually supervised your work closely, at college you will have to take responsibility for your own study. There will be other problems you are likely to meet.

Coping with loneliness and strangeness

When you get to college you are likely to be hit by the strangeness and loneliness, or by an exaggerated state of euphoria that you are at last free from the shackles of home and school. Perhaps you will wonder whether you will be able to cope with the work because the other students appear to be cleverer and more confident than you. It may take time to shake off these feelings, but don't think you are different: most students will feel the same way at first, however cool they may appear.

Lack of feedback about progress

You are likely to be upset by the lack of knowledge about how you are getting on with your studies. At school you probably had your work returned fairly promptly, so you had some knowledge of the results of your study, the feedback which is necessary for effective learning. In higher education this may not so readily be provided and you may find it difficult to discover how you are getting on. Ask yourself questions and check with books and lecture handouts, or use a friend or tutor to help.

Procrastination

You are likely to become a victim of your own procrastination rituals, so try to get down to work as soon as you close the door of your room. Don't try to find reasons or excuses for not studying.

Revising

You may be upset by an awareness that you are not revising enough. Set a regular time for revising, say once a week, but things you don't understand should not be avoided and must be revised in any spare minute. Try to write brief notes on all such difficult topics on small cards or paper, keep them in your pocket or handbag and refer to them in any spare moment, anywhere.

Remembering

You are likely to be upset by an awareness that you can't remember things you have learnt. The best way is to try to teach the things you can't understand or remember to someone else, perhaps another student or a friend, then let your friend do the same. You will then both become 'givers' as well as 'getters' in the course of learning together and since this becomes a rewarding experience for you both it will also help you to study.

Writing essays

You may encounter writing blocks, especially when you try to begin long essays or dissertations. Begin by writing brief sketches of your essay, quotations and references on scraps of paper, together with any suitable cuttings or illustrations, and collect all these by means of a large spring clip hung on the wall of your room, or have a large envelope or file easily at hand, into which you tumble any scraps of information which may come in useful. If it is a large assignment, use several clips or file information under different headings. Then, when you have a large collection, sort them out in your spare time so the material fits the intended outline of your essay. You will find that half the battle with your writing block is over.

This is the time to have a spell of conscious relaxation, to rest in a stage of passive awareness to clear your mind so that you are ready for the final stage of writing. Try it. It really works.

Seek help if you are in difficulties

Don't struggle on by yourself. Share your problems with a friend, your tutor or the counsellor before your anxieties affect your feelings of well-being, your work and your health.

7

Calming massage

Massage is one of the oldest forms of healing and is a supreme pleasure enjoyed by almost everyone. But although parents are prepared to stroke, pat, cuddle their babies and instinctively know that this is essential for their health and comfort, older children and adults miss out on this calming reassuring experience. We live in a touch deprived society, yet there is plenty of evidence to show how valuable this form of physical contact can be to reduce tension. Even stroking a pet has been shown to induce measurable changes, lowering blood pressure and pulse rate (although this is rather a poor substitute for the benefit of human contact).

Physically, massage improves the circulation of the skin, reduces the effects of fatigue and relieves aching muscles after strenuous activity. But valuable though these benefits are, it is the psychological effects that are so remarkable and rewarding for both giver and receiver. It has long been known that massage can soothe someone who is troubled, calm those who are over-excited, comfort those who are disturbed and help those who find it difficult to sleep. It is a way of conveying care and affection, of paying kindly attention to the needs of the one being massaged, and it gives the kind of reassurance that can only be conveyed by touch.

The skin is the largest and most sensitive organ in the body. Just below its surface are millions of tiny nerve endings which are responsive to touch: to pressure, warmth, cold or pain. These are the receptors and when they are stimulated they send nerve messages to the brain. If the sensation is perceived as painful, the message received is one of alarm and the body tenses for action. If the touch is reassuring and comfortable the message received is that all is well and there is no need to get geared up for action. A sense of inner peace develops. During the pleasurable sensation of stroking temperature in the anterior section of the hypothalamus (the centre in the brain dealing with emotions) is lowered and this is accompanied by relaxation.

Massage is skin speaking to skin and we all have our individual touch, like our own voice and personality. Some are heavy handed or awkward, others are quick and restless, some stroke with a diffident feathery touch and others in a way that is mechanical and insensitive, but some have a natural caring and tender touch that responds to the needs of the receiver. However, everyone can develop sensitive healing hands and can help children, partners and friends to enjoy the relaxation and feelings of well-being provided by massage. An added bonus is that it helps the giver to feel calm too.

The kind of massage I am describing is not concerned with medical treatment which should only be given by someone fully qualified and under the direction of a physician, but simple massage which can be given by anyone, even children (who are often very good indeed at it). There are only a few techniques and basic rules involved and you will soon develop your own successful methods.

The best way to learn is on yourself so that you can discover the kind of touch and technique that suits you best. It will also help you if you have no one to give you massage.

Self-massage – techniques

HANDS

This massage will help to keep your hands supple and dextrous, is useful before a musical performance, and as a break when you have been typing, writing or doing any intricate manual activity. It also helps you to develop sensitive hands for when you give massage to someone else.

1 Rub your hands together and wring them firmly, feeling the front and back of each hand.

2 Knead the palm of one hand with the thumb of the other. Make firm circular pressing movements.

3 Smooth your hand between thumb and fingers of the other hand as if you were smoothing on a glove.

4 Rub your hands briskly and fast, with palms facing. Gradually change to a slow lingering movement, feeling every part of each hand touching as it moves. Become aware of the sensation, then slow down to a stop.

5 Shake your hands loose then rest them relaxed and still on your lap.

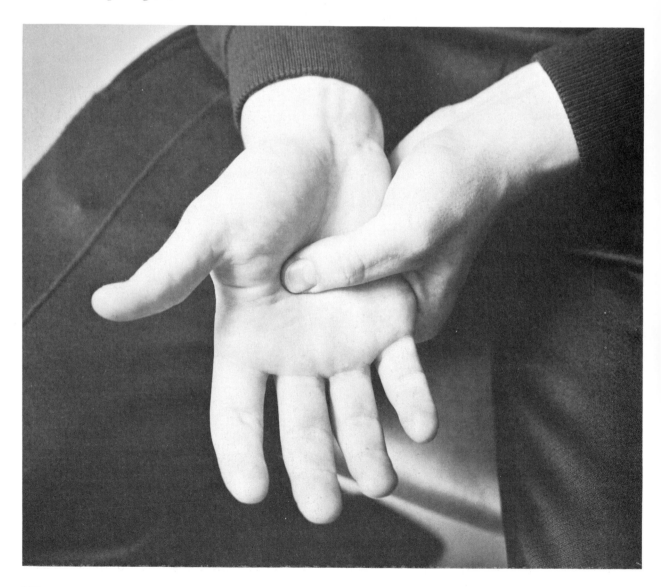

LEGS

This will relieve some of the fatigue and an aching in leg muscles after activity or long periods of standing, and is fine when you come in tired after shopping or after strenuous athletic activity. It is also useful to relax muscles in preparation for a sports event. It will help you to learn to mould your hands to the contours of parts of the body when you give massage.

This massage is not suitable for anyone with varicose veins.

1 Sit with one foot supported on a chair or stool, the knee bent. Grasp the ankle with both hands. Move your hands up towards the knee, keeping them in close contact so that there is no air space in between. Do this firmly as if you were straightening a long sock. As you reach the knee with the fingers stroke firmly behind it.

2 Give some squeezing and kneading movements to the sides and top of the thigh. Find out what pressure and which movements feel best.
3 Do the same to the other leg, then finish with a good shaking of the calves and then the thighs. (This is useful to loosen up before athletic events.)

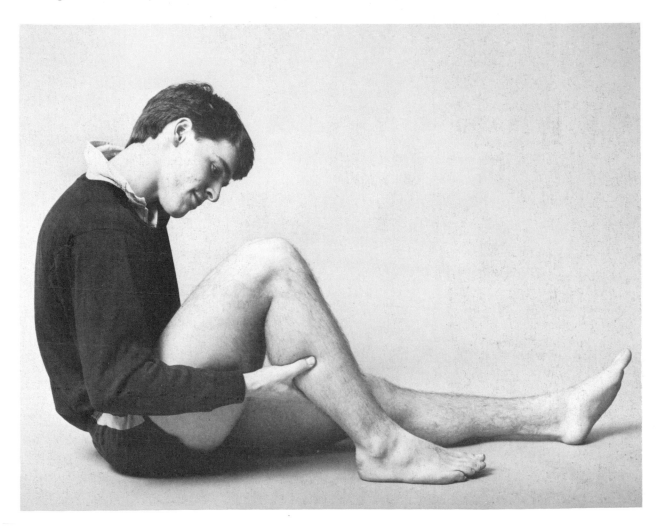

HEAD TAPPING and PALMING

The brisk tapping can relieve tension in the scalp muscles and it will help when you feel down or depressed. The palming will rest your eyes and help you to relax after a long spell of intense studying or whenever your eyes feel tired.

1 Sit upright looking forward. With the tips of your bent fingers tap quickly all over the top of your scalp: a brisk light movement like rain falling. Then continue tapping over the sides of your head, your forehead, then finish on the top again. Notice the different pressure you require for different parts.

2 Sit still for a moment aware of the tingling sensation. Then lean forward with your elbows on your knees or table and rest your head on your hands. The heels of your hands rest on the cheeks and the palms cover your closed eyes without pressing on them. Stay in the darkness like this for a short while until you feel rested.

FACE

Use this massage before you begin a relaxation session. It helps you to relieve tension in the worry muscles and will often allay an impending headache. Give yourself this massage whenever you feel uptight and before social occasions when you want to look at ease.

Notice the kind of pressure and the special techniques you like best so that you can use these later when you give massage to someone else.

1 Rub your hands all over your face with large circular movements, keeping the whole of your hand in contact with the skin.
2 With your fingertips, make small circular movements over your forehead, paying especial attention to any tender spots by the temples. Progress downwards to the cheeks. Make circular movements around the mouth to loosen tight lips.

3 Close your eyes. Place your hands so that fingertips meet in the middle of your forehead. Smooth very gently sideways and outwards towards the temples (your little fingers move gently over your closed eyes).
4 Place one hand across your forehead so that the whole of your hand is in contact. Smooth upwards from the bridge of the nose to the hairline (or over the top of your head to the back of the neck if the hair style allows). Do the same with the other hand, moving one hand after the other rhythmically. Always keep one hand in contact.

Rest your hands on your lap, stay still and relaxed, and become aware of the sensation of your relaxed face.

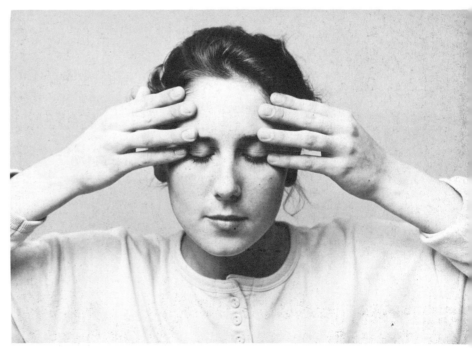

NECK

Stress quickly affects the neck muscles and you may find little knots of aching tension at the back of your neck. This massage can relieve this tension, pinpoint the painful spots, and will often relieve a headache.

When you have finished, move your head easily in all directions. Remember how heavy your head is and how hard the muscles have to work if you hold it badly. Then try to improve your head posture, especially if you are working on computers or studying with your head thrust forward. Give yourself neck massage at intervals as you work and try not to slouch because this affects your head position and causes strain.

First check up on tension in your neck muscles; grasp the back of your neck firmly with one hand and thrust your head forward; feel how this makes the muscles go hard and tense; move your head to a good easy position until you feel the difference when the muscles are more relaxed.

1 With the tips of your middle fingers make circular pressing movements along the base of the skull, beginning below and behind your ears gradually moving towards the centre at the back of your neck. Continue these movements down each side of your neck close to the spine. Experiment with the pressure until you find what gives you most relief.

2 Using the whole of one hand, make squeezing and lifting movements of the muscles at the back of your neck.

3 When you have finished, sit with your neck stretched taller than usual: don't let it compress so that it sinks towards your shoulders.

PARTNER MASSAGE
(by parent, friend or child)

General guidelines for giving a massage

Warmth – your hands and the room must be warm. If the receiver is to lie on the floor make sure there are no draughts and that there is a towel or rug to cover up the parts not being massaged.

Fingernails must be short or you will scratch. Any sharp rings should be removed.

Lubrication – if your hands are soft and dry there will be no need for lubrication. However, you may like to use a little baby oil or talcum powder to make your hands slip easily over the skin. Be careful about the oil though: put it in a safe place because if it is on the floor it can easily be spilt. Don't pour the oil on your partner, place a little on your own hands.

Feel relaxed before you begin – your feelings of tension are rapidly communicated by touch. Place your hands on your partner or child and stay quite still for a moment, saying to yourself 'Relax', 'Be calm', as you breathe out slowly. This not only helps you but will convey an immediate signal of quiet and relaxation to your partner.

Don't talk – once you have both got settled, avoid any conversation. This session is for feeling not for talking.

Mind your own back – your posture is important so that you avoid back strain. Move from your hips or ankles with as straight a back as possible. If you are giving massage on the floor, kneel beside your partner on a small cushion and sway backwards and forwards without bending your back. If you are doing it on a bed, sit on the edge rather than leaning forward. An improvised massage table, using a long dining or kitchen table, well-padded, is useful.

Keep your movements rhythmical – using music as a background may help you, but be careful about this. Your choice might disturb your partner and may distract you from sensitive feeling and communication. However, sometimes it is great fun to be accompanied by suitable music.

Keep your hands relaxed and sensitive moulding them to the contour of the body. Techniques are not important so long as you and the receiver enjoy it and the massage is comfortable. You will soon select the movements that have the desired effect.

In general, start with some deep purposeful stroking, avoiding an aimless wandering of the hands, then go on to light stroking away from the heart, in the direction of the flow of hairs to induce relaxation. At no time should it be painful.

'Quickie' massage can be done anywhere, without removing any clothes. You can help a weary teenager struggling with homework by giving a quick massage of hands. A brief forehead stroking, head stroking, neck

massage, shoulder massage will lower tension at any time, almost anywhere, and may avert a headache or explosion of rage. And it indicates that you care.

Longer massage – if you are giving a longer spell of general massage, take the telephone off the hook and keep the house as quiet as possible. When you have finished, cover up your partner and leave time for resting afterwards.

Teach your child to give you massage – it will be a splendid education for him or her and lovely for you. Reward the child with lots of 'Oohs and Ahs . . . that's lovely' and a hug when it is over.

If you are massaging a young child, keep the session short at first. It is particularly useful before bedtime to help quieten down an excited child or when the child is frightened.

Massage must never be painful – don't massage for long on one spot. Keep moving.

Contraindications – never massage over a rash, varicose veins, or open wounds, and if the child has a temperature keep him or her covered and stroke only over the bedclothes or over the head.

Partner massage – techniques

HANDS

This is a quick way to relieve tension in a partner's hands, especially after long periods of writing or when dexterity is important, such as before a musical performance. It is delightful as a 'quickie' to give comfort and reassurance and is useful when other forms of massage would be inappropriate.

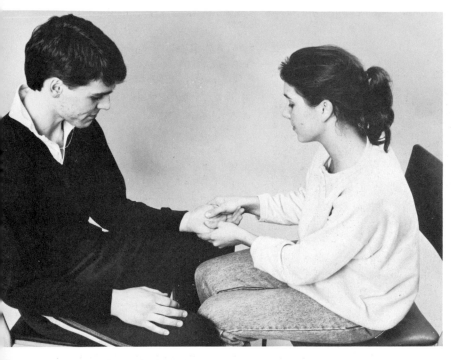

1 Rest your partner's hand, palm upwards, on both of yours. With your thumbs make firm circular pressing movements on all the fleshy parts of the palm and base of the thumb.
2 Turn the hand over and stroke from each fingertip to the back of the hand, then between the bones to the wrist. Do the same with each finger.

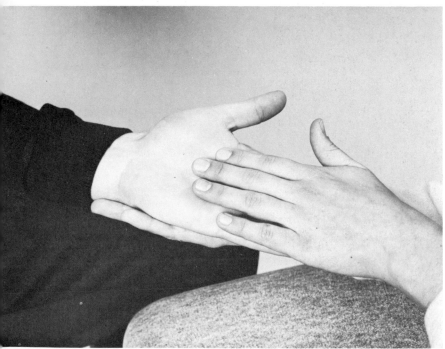

3 Finish by resting your partner's hand sandwiched between yours. Stay quite still for a moment, becoming aware of the warmth, then slowly stroke with both hands from wrist to fingertips. This is a lingering soothing stroking.

FACE

Face muscles quickly reflect emotional states and they soon show signs of stress if someone is tense or worried. Face massage followed by forehead massage induces a sense of general relaxation and conveys feelings of care and affection. This massage is particularly useful for giving reassurance, say, to a sick or unhappy child.

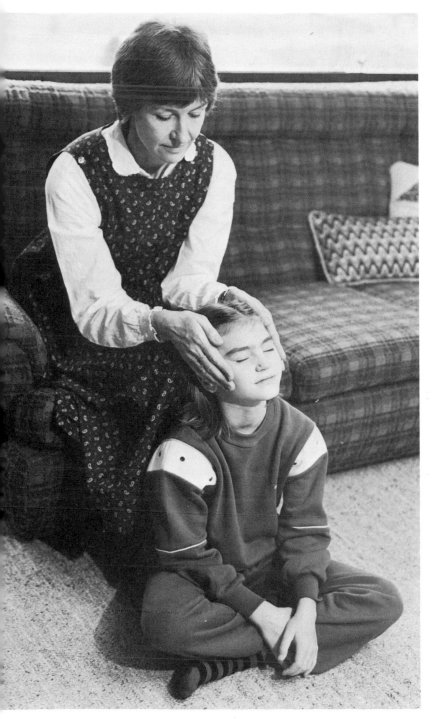

1 Sit on a chair with the child sitting in front of you on a cushion or a low stool, and her back supported against your legs. Lean forward, cup her face in your hands and stroke from the chin up to the top of the head. Feel the exact shape of her face as your hands mould to the contours.

Invent your own techniques like making gentle circling movements over the face, lips and ears. If the hair style allows, continue over the top of the head.

2 Most children (and adults) enjoy having their hair stroked and having some massage for the scalp. With your fingertips brush your hand firmly through the hair beginning at the back of the neck and moving over the scalp. Make some circular movements with your fingertips especially on the top of the scalp. Then move in the other direction from the front to the back of the head.

FOREHEAD

This is a delightful way to help a partner relax after a tiring day or when a headache is on the way. It often produces an astonishing change in appearance and the partner quickly changes from looking and feeling tense to looking peaceful and calm. Your own feeling of relaxation is important before you start the massage so that you convey the message 'relax'.

Starting positions

a) Partner sits on a chair with eyes closed and you stand behind, leaning forward so that your partner's head can rest back against you.

b) Partner sits on a low stool or cushion while you sit behind on a chair, while your partner's back rests against your knees.

1 Place your hands on your partner's forehead with fingertips touching in the centre. Stay still for a moment for you both to feel relaxed. Stroke smoothly and gently outwards to the temples. Keep the stroking slow and rhythmical (a rapid or jerky movement conveys messages of tension).

An alternative method is to place one hand across your partner's forehead and stroke outwards to the opposite temple. Without losing contact do the same with the other hand moving to the opposite side. Use whichever method suits your partner best.

2 Place one hand across the forehead and stroke upwards from the ridge of the nose to the hairline. Repeat with the other hand.

When it is time to finish, signal this by keeping your hand still on the forehead saying to yourself 'Relax'. Your partner should stay still for a moment before opening the eyes, becoming aware of the sensation of a relaxed forehead.

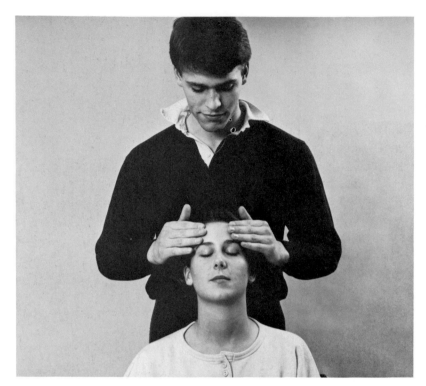

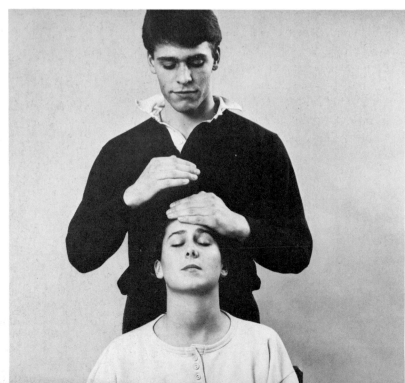

SHOULDERS

Many people experience tension and aching in shoulders when they have been on edge for some time. This massage will relieve some of the aching and reduce the tension. It can be a 'quickie' massage done over clothes at any time, but it is better with skin to skin contact.

Starting position
Sit on a chair with your partner sitting on a cushion or stool in front of you, the head supported on hands, elbows resting on knees.

1 Place your hands on top of the shoulders, so that your fingers are just over the top and your palms in contact with the skin at the back. Reach down with your thumbs and roll the skin upwards fairly firmly. Then make some kneading and squeezing movements using the whole of your hand. Keep to muscle, don't press on bone. Do this as deeply as your partner enjoys.

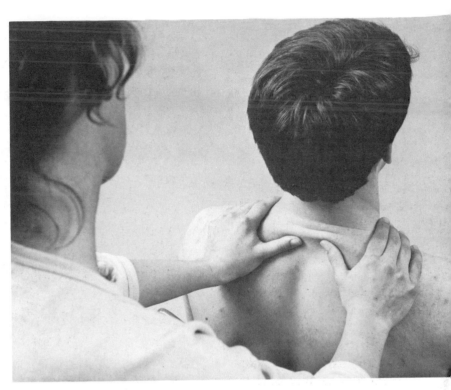

2 With your fingertips make circular pressing movements where the spots ache. Keep moving from place to place, being sure never to cause any pain by your movements.
    Finish with lingering smoothing massage down the neck and over the shoulders down the outside of the arms.

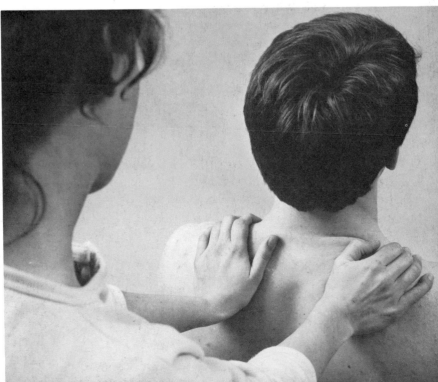

BACK

Back massage is probably the most delightful and effective way to help someone relax, and if given sensitively it will make the giver feel relaxed as well. Most adults and children enjoy a good back massage and it is particularly useful for someone who finds it difficult to get off to sleep.

PROPS – two large towels, a rug, two pillows, talc or oil.

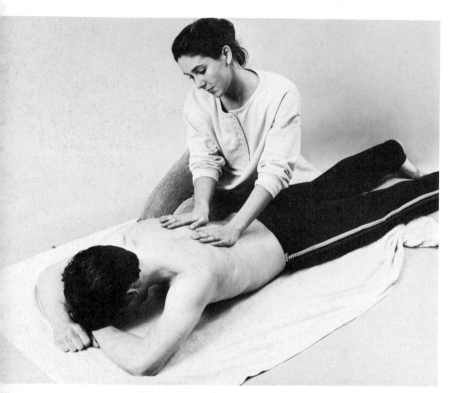

Make sure the room is warm and free from draughts.

Starting position
The receiver lies face downwards on the floor, on a bed, or on a padded table, with one pillow under the abdomen (to avoid an arched tense back) and the other under the ankles. There is usually no need for one under the head, but have a clean towel to rest on. The head rests on the hands, or it can be turned sideways.

The giver either kneels on the floor or stands at the side of the bed, one foot forward. If the bed is low, sit on the side of the bed. It is usually best to begin with some firm movements, changing gradually to lighter relaxing ones.

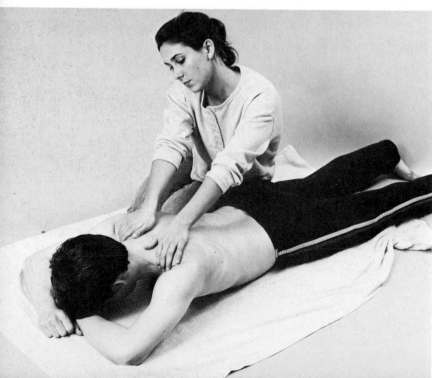

1 *Firm stroking* – place both hands at the base of the spine with fingers pointing upwards and the whole of your hand in contact. Working alongside the spine (but not on it) smooth firmly up towards the shoulders and over the top. Mould your hands exactly to the contours of the back. You can see the skin rolling ahead of your hands. Do this several times.

2 *Fanning out* – begin at the base of the spine as before but fan out your stroking as you move upwards so that you massage first towards the outer shoulders and then out to the sides of the back. This is still quite a firm movement.

You can add some kneading or lifting movements if it suits you both. Massaging must never be uncomfortable.

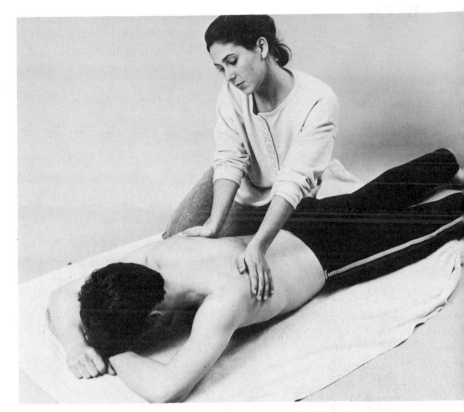

3 *Relaxed stroking* – starting at the neck, stroke softly with one relaxed hand down the length of the back. As you reach the base of the spine, and before you lose contact do the same on the other side with the other hand. Hands move alternately, lightly and rhythmically with a lingering movement. Always have one hand in contact. Feel as relaxed as you can yourself and convey a message of tranquillity through your hands. Gradually get slower . . . slower . . . and lighter, until you stop.

Stay for a moment with your hand still on the back. Pull a blanket over your partner and go away quietly, leaving him to relax fully.

4 *An alternative alert ending* – if this is only a short session and the receiver has to be alert again, end with gentle but stimulating slapping movements all over the back.

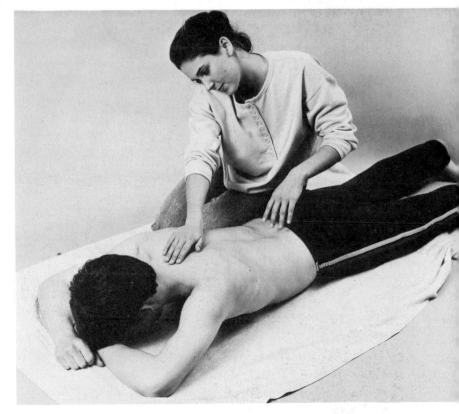

FOOT

In the soles of the feet there are thousands of nerve endings and for many people foot massage is particularly pleasant and relaxing; as long as the massage is firm and purposeful it won't be ticklish. Foot massage will relieve tired feet and, coupled with some exercise, will maintain or even improve suppleness in the feet and ankles.

Starting positions
a) The child sits on a chair with one leg resting on a stool.
b) The child lies on the floor either facing up or facing downwards, whichever is most comfortable.
c) You both sit on a settee, the child with legs resting along it. Parent faces child and massages each foot in turn.

1 Support the top of the foot with one hand and with the heel of the other massage firmly the sole of the foot. Then with your thumbs make firm circular movements over the sole.

2 Massage the top of the foot. With your thumbs make circular movements between the bones of the foot.
3 Work the joints carefully: take each tip of the toes in turn and move it in a circular direction. Move the whole foot up and down and finish by making a big circle of the ankle.
4 End the session with smooth stroking of the top and sole of the foot, both hands working together from the ankle to toe tips.

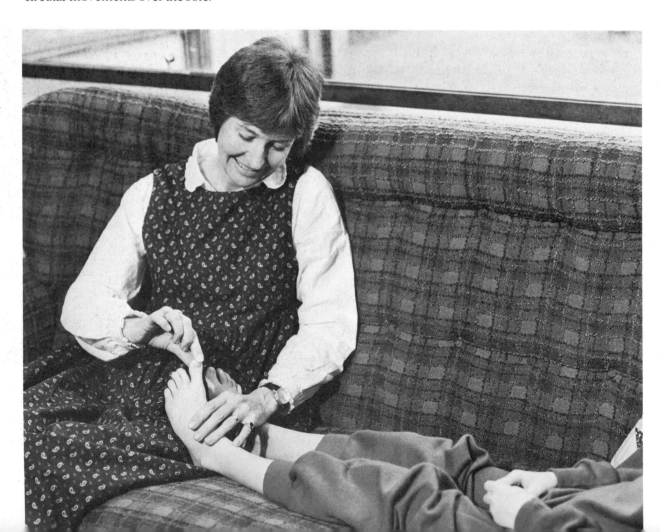

MASSAGE GIVEN BY CHILDREN

This gives children an introduction to the techniques of simple massage and also gives them the opportunity to show affection towards their parents through touch. This is particularly soothing for mothers when they are tired and tense.

The child should be rewarded by an appreciation of the calming effects produced by this massage.

Older children could give soothing massage to the baby of the family. It often settles a fretful infant and gives the reassurance and caring physical contact that is beneficial for development.

Any of the techniques described earlier can be adapted. The easiest ones are for face, hands and shoulders.

1 *Face* – parent lies on the floor with the child kneeling behind. Stroking movements begin beneath the chin then follow the jaw line up to the temples. After a while this is followed by gentle stroking across the forehead.

This can also be done with the parent sitting on a chair with the child standing behind.

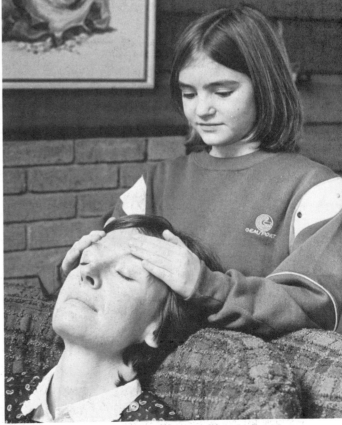

2 *Shoulders* – parent sits on a low chair or stool. The child stands behind and strokes firmly over the shoulders and follows this with squeezing or picking up movements. The parent should indicate movements that feel particularly good.

3 *Hands* – parent's hand rests palm upwards. The child gives circular pressings with the thumbs and follows this with stroking from wrist to fingers.

4 *Foot* – parent rests on settee or floor and child sits facing alongside. Use any of the techniques shown earlier but if the parent is particularly ticklish, begin with toe circling and stroking the top of the ankle.

Appendix 1
Suggestions for music for dance

Many teachers will have their own ideas for music, but here are some suggestions for those who want help.

General selections

1 *Listen and Move* – beginning with pieces suitable for infants and Junior age children it leads up to music appropriate for older children. (1 × 12in record and guide, Northcote House Publishers).

2 *Listen, Move and Dance* – this contains sections for:
   a) quick and light movements
   b) quick and strong movements
   c) slow and light movements
   d) slow and strong movements
   e) electronic sound patterns.
   (Record, EMI).

3 *A Pageant of Dances* – various themes for older children (1 × 12in record and guide; 1 cassette and guide; Northcote House Publishers).

4 Kraftwerk, *The Man Machine* – electronic music for robots (EMI).

5 *Simon and Garfunkel's Greatest Hits* – floating, light sustained movements, some shaky and loose.

6 Andrew Lloyd Webber, *Variations*.

Specific movements

1 *Strong movements*
   a) *Carmen*, Bizet: 'Toreador Song'
   b) *The Planets*, Holst: 'Mars the Bringer of War'
   c) *Carmina Burana*, Orff: 'Fortuna Imperatrix Mundi'
   d) *Swan Lake*, Tchaikowski: 'Waltz in A Major'
   e) *The Planets*, Holst: 'Jupiter, the Bringer of Jollity'

2 *Floating, light, sustained movements*
   a) *Casse-noisette*, Tchaikowski: 'Valse des fleurs'

b) Chopin: 'Prelude Op. 28. No 16'
       'Nocturne Op. 15. No 2'
       'Waltz in B Minor, Op. 69'
c) *Carnival of the Animals*, Saint-Saens: 'Aquarium and The Swan'
d) *Capriol suite*, Warlock: 'Pieds en l'air'
e) *Chariots of Fire*, Vangelis

3 *Shaking, shivering, loose movements*
a) *Capriol Suite*, Warlock: 'Bransles and Mattachins'
b) *Casse-noisette*, Tchaikowski: 'Dance Chinoise'
c) Chopin: 'Waltz in E flat, Op. 18'
d) *Carnival of the Animals*, Saint-Saens: 'The Aviary'

4 *Jerky movements*
a) *Capriol Suite*, Warlock: 'Tordion'
b) *Swan Lake*, Tchaikowski: 'Dance of the Little Swans'
c) *Spanish Flea*, Herb Alpert and the Tijuana Brass

—— Appendix 2 ——
Some other methods

Note: It is advisable to enclose SAE when requesting information

ALEXANDER TECHNIQUE   A process of self-education of good body use and posture. Classes and individual instruction: The Society for Teachers of the Alexander Technique, 3 Albert Court, Kensington Gore, London SW7.

AUTOGENIC TRAINING   A series of simple mental exercises designed to help body and mind relax. Individual instruction: Centre for Autogenic Training, 15 Fitzroy Square, London W1P 5HQ.

CHINESE MARTIAL ARTS   Judo can give children confidence when they learn self-defence and self-discipline: The Chinese Culture Arts Association, 90 Aldbanks, Dunstable, Bedfordshire.

LAURA MITCHELL METHOD OF PHYSIOLOGICAL RELAXATION   This involves learning how to change the positions of tension one by one to the exactly opposite positions and to feel the result in each joint. Information about books and cassettes: Miss Laura Mitchell, MCSP, Dip TP, 8 Gainsborough Gardens, Well Walk, Hampstead, London NW3 1BJ.

MARGARET MORRIS MOVEMENT   Classes for children as well as adults: special features include mobility of the spine, breathing exercises, dance-like strengthening movements and relaxation: The National Association of the Margaret Morris Movement, Suite 3/4, 39 Hope Street, Glasgow G2 6AG.

BIOFEEDBACK   Information and apparatus from: Aleph One, The Old Courthouse, Bottisham, Cambridge.

LOOK AFTER YOURSELF CLASSES   These classes for adults include exercise, health education and relaxation and are held in many parts of the United Kingdom: Health Education Council, 78 New Oxford Street, London WC1.

RELAXATION FOR LIVING   This organisation is a charitable trust which promotes the teaching of physical relaxation to combat stress. There are classes in various parts of the UK, correspondence courses and training courses for teachers. There are leaflets and relaxation cassettes for sale:

The Hon. Secretary, Relaxation for Living, 29 Burwood Park Road, Walton-on-Thames, Surrey KT12 5LH.

MEDITATION   It is better for children to use only the very simple techniques of thought diversion outlined in this book. Later, those who are ready to go further can obtain information from Transcendental Meditation, Mentmore Towers, Leighton Buzzard, Bucks.

YOGA   Hatha Yoga usually includes relaxation and there are classes for children as well as adults. Information from: The British Wheel of Yoga, 445 High Road, Ilford, Essex IG1 1TR.

Further reading

Child development

BAYARD R. & BAYARD J. (1981) *Help! I've got a Teenager!* Exley Publications.

BROOK C. G. D. (1985) *All About Adolescence*, John Wiley.

COLEMAN J. C. (ed.) (1979) *The School Years*, Methuen.

CRABTREE, J. (1983) *An A–Z of Children's Emotional Problems*, Unwin Paperbacks.

CRATTY (1972) *Perceptual and motor development in infants and children*, Prentice Hall.

DALTON K. (1978) *Once a Month* (menstruation), Fontana Paperbacks.

FOGELMAN K. R. (1983) *Growing up in Great Britain*, Macmillan.

GABRIEL J. (1966) *Children Growing Up*, University of London Press.

HURLOCK E. *Child Development*, McGraw-Hill.

KAHN J. H. (1967) *Human Growth and the Development of Personality*, Pergamon Press.

MOLLAN C. (1979) *Children First: A Source Book for Parents and Other Professionals*, The Women's Press.

MUSSEN P., CONGER J. & KAGAN J. (1978) *Child Development and Personality*, McGraw-Hill.

ODLAM D. (1978) *Adolescence*, Wayland Publishers.

OPEN UNIVERSITY (1982) *Childhood 5–10 years*, Open University, Milton Keynes.

OPIE I. O. & P. O. (1969) *The Lore and Language of Schoolchildren*, Clarendon Press.

PRINGLE KELLMER M. (1974) *The Needs of Children*, Hutchinson.

RARICK C. L. (1973) *Physical Activity, Human Growth and Development*, Academic Press.

SILBERMAN M. & WHEELAN S. A. (1980) *How to Discipline without Feeling Guilty: Assertive Relationships with Children*, Research Press.

STONE J. & CHURCH J. (1957) *Childhood and Adolescence*, Random Press.

TANNER J. T. (1978 2nd ed.) *Education and Physical Growth*, Hodder & Stoughton.

TANNER J. T. (1962) *Growth at Adolescence*, Blackwell Scientific Publications.

Stress and relaxation

BARNES B. & COLQUHOUN I. (1984) *The Hyperactive Child: What the Family Can Do*, Thorsons.

BENSON H. (1963) *The Relaxation Response*, William Morrow.

CANNON W. B. (1963) *Bodily Changes in Pain, Hunger, Fear and Rage*, Harper & Row.

CARR J. (1985) *Helping Your Handicapped Child* (this includes a useful section on getting over phobias and could be useful to all parents), Penguin Handbooks.

COLEMAN V. (1980) *Stress Control*, Pan.

ELLIOTT M. (1985) *Preventing Sexual Assault*, Bedford Square Press.

FINK D. H. (1954) *Release from Nervous Tension*, Allen & Unwin.

GELLHORN E. (1967) *Principles of Autonomic Somatic Integration*, University of Minnesota Press.

GRAY J. (1971) *The Psychology of Fear and Stress*, World University Library.

HEWITT J. (1985) *Relaxation*, Hodder & Stoughton.

JACOBSEN E. (1962) *You Must Relax*, McGraw-Hill.

LEVITT E. E. (1968) *The Psychology of Anxiety*, Staples Press.

MADDERS J. (1981) *Stress and Relaxation*, Martin Dunitz.

McQUADE W. & ACKMAN A. (1973) *Stress: How To Stop Your Mind Killing Your Body*, Arrow Books.

MITCHELL L. (1977) *Simple Relaxation*, John Murray.

ROSA K. R. (1976) *Autogenic Training*, Victor Gollancz.

RUSSELL P. (1978) *Meditation: Paths to Tranquillity*, BBC Publications

RUTTER M. (1982) *Helping Troubled Children*, Penguin Books.

SELYE H. (1956) *The Stress of Life*, McGraw-Hill.

SELYE H. (1978) *Stress without Strain*, Hodder & Stoughton.

TODMAN R. (1979) *Social Causes of Illness*, Souvenir Press.

VARNA V. P. (ed.) (1973) *Stresses in Children*, Hodder & Stoughton.

WEEKES C. (1962) *Self-help for Your Nerves*, Angus & Robertson.

WOLFF S. (1981) *Children under Stress*, Penguin Books.

Studying

GIBBS G. (1981) *Teaching Students to Learn*, Open University Press, Milton Keynes.

KJELL R. & WANKOWSKI J. (1981) *Helping Students to Learn at University*, Sigma Forlag, Bergen.

MARSHALL L. A. & ROWLAND F. (1981) *A Guide to Learning Independently*, Longman.

ROWNTREE D. (1976) *Learn How to Study*, Macdonald.

Physical education: posture, dance, sport

BARKER S. (1982) *The Alexander Technique*, Bantam Books.

BARLOW W. (ed.) (1978) *More talk of Alexander: Aspects of the Alexander Principle*, Victor Gollancz.

BROSNAM B. (1982) *Yoga for Handicapped People*, Souvenir Press.

D.E.S. (1980) *Movement: Physical Education in the Primary Years*, HMSO.

FENTON J. V. (1973) *Choice of Habit: Poise, Free Movement, and the Practical Use of the Body*, Macdonald & Evans.

KANE J. E. (ed.) (1975) *Psychological Aspects of Physical Education and Sport*, Routledge & Kegan Paul.

PRESTON-DUNLOP V. (1980) *Handbook for Dance in Education*, Macdonald & Evans.

SETTERLIND SVEN (1978) *Introducing Relaxation Training in Swedish Schools*, Department for Sport Psychology, Orebro University, Sweden.

SHREEVES R. (1979) *Children Dancing*, Ward Lock.

SYER J. & CONNOLLY C. (1982) *Sporting Mind, Sporting Body: Athletes' Guide to Mental Training*, Cambridge University Press.

Massage

AUCKETT A. (1981) *Baby Massage*, Hill of Content Publishing Co, Melbourne.

DOWNING G. (1972) *The Massage Book*, Penguin Books.

MONTAGUE A. (1978) *Touching*, Harper & Row.

WEST O. (1983) *The Magic of Massage*, Century Publishing.

WOOD E. & BECKER P. D. (1981) *Beard's Massage*, W. B. Saunders.

Disorders associated with stress

ANDERSON J. V. (1981) *Diabetes*, Martin Dunitz.

BARNES B. & COLQUHOUN I. (1984) *The Hyperactive Child: What the Family Can Do*, Thorsons.

KNIGHT A. (1981) *Asthma and Hay Fever*, Martin Dunitz.

MACKIE R. (1983) *Eczema and Dermatitis*, Martin Dunitz.

WILKINSON M. (1982) *Migraine and Headaches*, Martin Dunitz.

WORKMAN E., HUNTER J. & JONES V. A. (1984) *The Allergy Diet*, Martin Dunitz.

Cassettes

'I CAN RELAX.' A cassette recording by Jane Madders for young children (4 to 10 years) is based on this book. The first lesson is short and intended to be fun. It includes vigorous physical activity to release tension followed by quiet control. The second lesson has more activities, includes some visualisation and full relaxation. The third lesson (on the second side) is more advanced, there are no activities and the full relaxation can be practised sitting in a chair, lying on the ground or in bed, or even sitting in the car on a long journey.

The cassette can be obtained from Relaxation for Living, 29 Burwood Park Road, Walton-on-Thames, Surrey KT12 5LH6.

A cassette for older children and adults, 'SELF-HELP RELAXATION', can be obtained from the same address.

___ Appendix 4 ___
Useful addresses

Someone to talk to is a comprehensive (but rather expensive) book compiled by The Sunday Times and published by Routledge & Kegan Paul. It includes addresses of a great many organisations and individuals offering help. If you need help and want someone to talk to it is well worth while getting the book from the library, or contact your local health education department: they will probably have it or be able to give you the information you seek.

PARENTS ANONYMOUS   If you feel you are near battering point look in your local telephone directory for the number to ring. Sympathetic parents who understand the problems, and who have had further training, offer support on the telephone. If you cannot find a local number, ring the NSPCC or write to: Parents Anonymous, 6/9 Manor Gardens, Islington, London N7 6LA.

HANDICAPPED CHILDREN   There are several organisations offering help and advice to parents of handicapped children:
   Kith and Kids, Bedford House, 35 Emerald Street, London WC1.
   MIND, National Association for Mental Health, 22 Harley Street, London W1N 2E.

HYPERACTIVE CHILDREN   Parents who are members receive regular newsletters, advice and information: HACSG (Hyper-active Children's Support Group), 59 Meadowside, Angmering, West Sussex BN16 4BW.

ECZEMA   National Eczema Society, 27 Doyle Gardens, London NW10 3DB.

GIFTED CHILDREN   National Association for Gifted Children, 27 John Adam Street, London WC2.

ANOREXIA   For parents and families involved with anorexia nervosa, Anorexic Aid, Priory Centre, Priory Road, High Wycombe, Bucks.

POST NATAL DEPRESSION   Association of Post Natal Illness, Queen Charlotte's Hospital, Goldhawk Road, London W4.

MIGRAINE   The British Migraine Association, 178 High Road, Byfleet, Weybridge, Surrey KT14 7ED.
The Migraine Trust, 45 Great Ormond Street, London WC1

THE NATIONAL CHILDREN'S BUREAU This organisation has under-taken long-term research into the growth and development of children and has published a number of reports and books and will give helpful information about these: National Children's Bureau, 8 Wakley Street, London EC1V 7QE.

MEDAU SOCIETY Classes for adults and children, 8B Robson House, Epsom KT17 1HH